Back Street Genius
The Story of Derek Tompkins
Part One
Shield Recording Studio

Dave Clemo
With
Roger Kinsey & Mavis Tompkins

First edition published in 2020

A catalogue number for this book is available from
The British Library

ISBN 978-1-913663-35-3

.

DEDICATION

This book is dedicated to the memory of Derek Tompkins and his legacy. He was innovative, inspirational and a major influence in the careers of several giants of the recording industry. He truly was a Back Street Genius.

WHAT THEY SAY ABOUT THE BOOK

'I'm more than impressed, there are some pieces on myself I'd forgotten about! You have done a great job. Derek would have been very proud of you all.'
Barry Noble (1960s Columbia Records recording star and lifelong friend of Derek & Mavis))

'Reading 'Back Street Genius' brought back so many personal memories of my first proper recording sessions. This book is a rollicking reminder of those early gigs in the area, and how we all just got on with it. If you've wondered what it was really like in those early days in a real recording studio, you will definitely enjoy this book!'
Bernie Marsden (guitarist with million selling rock band Whitesnake)

ACKNOWLEDGEMENTS

The authors would like to thank Sheila and the staff at Kettering Library for their help in making their volumes of the Northamptonshire Evening Telegraph and Northants Advertiser available for our research. Dave thinks that he must have looked at every page of every edition from 1962 to 1969! Some of the articles and images are taken from microfilm and are of less than perfect quality and for that we apologise.

We must also thank the many anonymous contributors to online websites devoted to 1950s and 1960s life and music. Their posts helped fill in the gaps in our knowledge. The Discogs website was another valuable resource. Some of the photographs in the book were copied from the internet and our thanks go to the original posters.

Clive Smith's excellent book 'It's Steel Rock & Roll to Me' is packed full of personal memories that added to our story and our thanks go to him for allowing us to use them.

We were also able to refer to Mavis' book 'Making the Best of it' for essential background information. She also made her extensive collection of photographs, records and memorabilia available.

Thanks to Ann & Ray Brett, Steve Fearn, Keith Sheffield, Alan Course, the late Peter Grantham, Robin Goodfellow, Bill Coleman, Nick Evans and Phil Dainty for agreeing to be interviewed for their memories.

The wonders of the internet enabled Roger Thory, Mike Benfield, Des Leonard and Barry Noble to add their memories by email. Our thanks go to them.

The contributors to the Derek Tompkins RIP Facebook page also deserve an honourable mention. Their posts and comments contained a mine of information. Our apologies go to anyone we may have missed out in the roll call.

The page was set up by Barry Hart a few years ago. He died before this project came to fruition. RIP.

INTRODUCTION BY MAVIS TOMPKINS

I think I can say my life with Derek has been similar to a roller coaster ride; a mix of promising anticipation coupled with the precarious apprehension of what might lie ahead, and a resolution to accept that enigmatic conclusion with fortitude and grace. Although it was at times a somewhat bumpy ride with many a hard knock on the way, we held on tight.

Derek and my late, much loved father had much in common. Both were inventive, enterprising, and enthusiastic in their mutual love of electrical engineering and methods of communication. This latter accomplishment led to Derek's emergence as a sound recording engineer.

As well as having a knowledgeable aptitude for designing and manufacturing Public Address equipment, he also built and equipped his own recording studios, beginning with Shield in Cambridge Street Kettering, and continuing with Beck in Lister Road, Wellingborough.

Music has always played a big part in our lives (excuse the pun) and we made countless friends among the musicians, vocalists and song writers who came our way. I have deeply valued these friendships through the years.

Derek's achievements together with the memories of those who were influenced in their lives by him will remain and endure.

Mavis Tompkins May 2020.

CONTENTS

Introduction		Page 1
Chapter 1	Recording Sound	Page 4
Chapter 2	In the Beginning	Page 10
Chapter 3	The Birth of the Q Men	Page 20
Chapter 4	1963	Page 32
Chapter 5	High Fidelity Vocals	Page 37
Chapter 6	The Windmill Club 1965	Page 46
Chapter 7	1966	Page 59
Chapter 8	In the News	Page 65
Chapter 9	Derek leaves the Q Men	Page 70
Chapter 10	Making Records	Page 74
Chapter 11	Recording at Shield Part 1	Page 83
Chapter 12	The Canadians	Page 89
Chapter 13	Barry Noble	Page 103
Chapter 14	Recording at Shield Part 2	Page 116
Chapter 15	The Tin Hat opens	Page 119
Chapter 16	Recording at Shield Part 3	Page 127
Chapter 17	Steve Fearn	Page 132
Chapter 18	Busy Busy Busy	Page 136
Chapter 19	Robin Goodfellow & Nick Evans	Page 143
Chapter 20	Diabolus and Skinny Cat	Page 150
Chapter 21	Pesky Gee/ Black Widow	Page 161
Chapter 22	The New Formula	Page 168
Chapter 23	John Deacon & The Opposition	Page 179
Chapter 24	1969	Page 181
Chapter 25	TV Times	Page 185
Chapter 26	Studio Success	Page 193
Chapter 27	The Breakup	Page 201
	RIP Alan Dobson	Page 205
	About the Authors	Page 207
Appendix1	Tin Hat dates	Page 209
Appendix2	Before they were famous	Page 230
	Other Books	Page 239

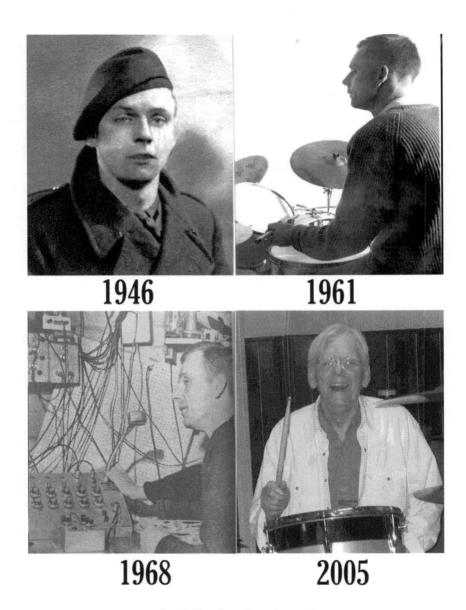

1946 1961

1968 2005

Derek Tompkins (1925 - 2013).

INTRODUCTION

These days we are surrounded by music. Hundreds of radio stations, each one playing 'the soundtrack to your life' are available at the touch of a button, 24 hours a day, 7 days a week, 365 days a year. There is so much recorded music available, far more than anyone could listen to even if they did nothing else from birth to death. Someone claimed that almost every piece of recorded music ever made is available in digital form somewhere.

It wasn't always so.

Sixty years ago, the world was a different place. The TV had two channels, BBC and ITV. The BBC broadcast three radio stations but pop music was restricted to the Light Programme until the advent of Radio 1 in 1967, and that might not have come about if it wasn't for the popularity of Radio Luxembourg and the pirate radio stations like Radio Caroline and Radio London.

'Saturday Club' was hosted by Brian Matthew on the Light Programme from 1957 until the late 1960s. The acts featured on the programme either played live or were pre recorded at the BBC Maida Vale studio. The other radio shows included 'Pick of the Pops', a single two hour long show on a Sunday afternoon and 'Two Way Family Favourites', a request show broadcast on Sunday lunchtimes.

A huge proportion of the records released were poor imitations of US chart hits not available here. For many years almost the only pop music shows on TV were 'Juke Box Jury' on the BBC, and 'Thank your Lucky Stars' on ITV.

The Musicians Union pressured the BBC to limit 'needle time' (the amount of recorded music played on air) in order to protect the interests of their members and had stopped US singers from touring the UK unless there was a reciprocal US tour by a UK based act.

After Lonnie Donegan kick started the Skiffle revolution in the mid 1950s thousands of young people learned to play guitar. Rock & Roll picked up the momentum. Every town in the UK had at least one pop group.

The London based music business played safe and promoted anodyne versions of American stars singing songs from Tin Pan Alley or covers of US hits. The offer of a recording contract was highly prized. Not every act had the chance to make a record for posterity.

The career path of the recording artistes was clearly defined. A single every three months followed by an album of their 'A' sides and 'B' sides, an end of the pier show in the summer, pantomime in the winter and one nighters on the various package tours that crisscrossed the country.

This cosy world changed in 1962 when The Beatles passed their audition and were given a contract to record on the Parlophone label. The music business would never be the same again.

Pop package tours: 1958 & 1962.

CHAPTER 1: RECORDING SOUND

The ability to capture, store and reproduce sound is a fairly recent event when set against the whole of human history. In the 1870s Alexander Graham Bell invented the telephone. It consisted of a device to capture a sound, a wire to transmit it along, and something to convert the electrical signal back into an audible form. This invention was quickly followed in 1878 by Edison's phonograph. For the first time in human history it was possible to hear music without the person playing it being present.

Other inventors made improvements to the original concept. In 1887 Emil Berliner invented the flat disc record. By the end of the 19th century it was possible to store and play back sounds using a system that used steel wire coiled around a cylinder.

In the 1920s two German inventors came up with a way to electronically amplify this recorded sound. It ushered in the era of the 'talkies'- movies with a soundtrack. The British Marconi Wireless Telegraphy Company bought the patent from the Germans. Marconi machines were used by the BBC throughout the 1930s.

Meanwhile a German chemist called Pfleumer patented the use of magnetised tape as a recording medium. Within a few years the German firm of AEG was marketing a tape recorder called the Magnetophon. At the outbreak of WW2, the audio quality of these machines was such that it was impossible to tell if a radio broadcast was live or recorded.

John T 'Jack' Mullin joined the US Army Signal Corps just before the outbreak of the war. In 1944 he was sent to England to help solve radio interference caused by the new radar installations. He used to spend most evenings listening to the radio. After the BBC shut down at midnight, he switched to a German radio station that played symphonic music. The music was taped but the quality was much better than the best available back in the US.

After the Liberation he was sent to Paris to help evaluate captured German electronic equipment. He heard about some Magnetophon tape recorders stored in a castle near Frankfurt. These machines were the ones used by that radio station.

He was able to obtain two of the recorders legally under war souvenir regulations. He stripped them down to their basic components and shipped them back to the US, a piece at a time. He also obtained 50 reels of audio tape, almost the entire stock available.

After demobilisation he returned to San Francisco and quickly rebuilt them. He demonstrated one of his machines at a meeting of the Institute of Radio Engineers in May 1946. Ampex heard it and hired him on the spot.

Jack Mullin with three Ampex machines.

Singer and film star Bing Crosby had a weekly syndicated radio show that went out live across the US. He wanted to pre-record his show so he could spend more time on the golf course. The radio station agreed on condition that the recordings were indistinguishable from the live broadcast.

Jack Mullin's tape recorder was exactly what Crosby wanted and he invested a significant amount of money in Ampex on condition that his firm BCE (Bing Crosby Enterprises) had the exclusive distribution rights.

Bing's regular band was led by a guitar playing genius called Les Paul. In 1949 Crosby gave him one of the early production Ampex machines and over the next couple of years Les Paul experimented and invented tape-based sound on sound recording by adding another record head. Together with his wife Mary Ford he recorded 'How High The Moon', a song that still sounds fresh almost 70 years later. He also put his name on Gibson's first solid electric guitar and was one of the pioneers of electronic effects like tape echo. He created all this groundbreaking music in the studio he built in his garage.

The post war years in the US were full of innovation and opportunity. Independent studio owners like Sam Phillips of Sun Records of Memphis and Berry Gordy of Tamla Motown in Detroit changed the music business forever.

Meanwhile back in the UK the years immediately following the end of the war were a time of rebuilding, rationing and austerity.

The BBC held the monopoly on radio and TV broadcasts. Those same German Magnetophon recorders that Ampex adapted were also used as the basis for the BBC's first post-war tape recorders. Domestic tape recorders didn't start appearing until the early 1950s and were mostly German brands like Grundig, Blaupunkt and Telefunken.

Radio was king. Before the Coronation of 1952 the television audience was miniscule. Very few households owned a gramophone and 78 rpm discs were luxury items. There was more likely to be a piano than a radiogram in the parlour.

The Music Industry of Tin Pan Alley was based around sales of sheet music and it wasn't until 1952 that the first record chart was published in the New Musical Express.

The sample of retailers that supplied the sales figures was very small.

The chart measured the popularity of a song rather than the sales of a record, so very often the top twenty might feature several versions of the same song.

The UK record companies enjoyed an unrivalled monopoly. They owned the studios and the record labels. Their recording contracts were loaded in favour of the company, and even the biggest selling artists were paid a tiny royalty. In addition- any breakages of the notoriously fragile shellac discs were paid for out of the artist's royalties. It was all very cosy and ripe for a recording revolution.

Someone said that teenagers didn't exist until the mid 1940s. Up until then they were either children, adolescents or young adults. When firms realised that teenagers had disposable income, they began marketing products specially aimed at them.

In the early 1950s Hollywood began making films like James Dean's 'Rebel Without A Cause' for the teen/young adult market.

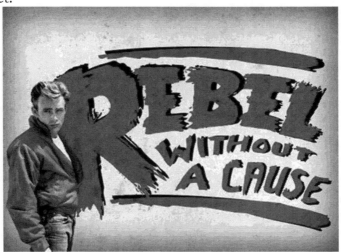

1956 was a pivotal year. The Suez Crisis was a humiliating defeat for the UK. Prime Minister Anthony Eden was forced to resign and was replaced by Harold Macmillan. Britain's empire began its slow decline.

ITV began broadcasting in London in September 1955 and in April 1956 ATV started broadcasting in the Midlands, with Granada starting a month or so later.

1956 was also the year when the first episodes of Hancock's Half Hour and TV talent show Opportunity Knocks began broadcasting.

In the US the best-selling records of 1956 were 'Heartbreak Hotel' and 'Don't Be Cruel' by Elvis Presley. 14-year-old Aretha Franklin had just recorded her first gospel album. Buddy Holly signed a three-year song writing contract with Decca and Elvis Presley's first LP was released by RCA Victor and Hollywood film star Marilyn Monroe married Arthur Miller.

In the UK the best-selling artists were Doris Day, Pat Boone and Frankie Laine. The biggest selling British artist was pianist Winifred Atwell.

The top selling music papers in the late 1950s.

CHAPTER 2: IN THE BEGINNING

Whenever recording studios are mentioned the first places that spring to mind are EMI's Abbey Road Studio in London or the Sun Recording Studio in Memphis. The more knowledgeable might be able to name Olympic Studio in Barnes where The Rolling Stones, Jimi Hendrix and a host of top groups recorded in the late 60s. Island Records' Basing Street Studio in West London was another with an impressive roster of hit records and in the early 70s residential studios like Richard Branson's Manor in Oxfordshire and Rockfield based in Monmouthshire became very popular. Queen's 'Bohemian Rhapsody' was recorded at Rockfield and is arguably the studio's most famous recording.

For every Abbey Road type Studio that produced records that sold in their millions there were dozens of smaller studios up and down the country that were set up to record the local talent. There's no doubt that the majority of the artistes that used them were amateurs who did so in order to make a record for posterity and semi-professionals who made demos to play to agents, or to interest the record companies. Very occasionally a recording session from one of these small studios resulted in a hit record.

This is the story of Derek Tompkins and Shield, the studio he set up in Kettering in the mid 1960s before moving to Wellingborough in 1969. He was a pioneer, and his studios were a training ground for at least two giants of the record industry and where future members of Queen and Whitesnake made early demos. For twenty years Derek ran the top studio in this corner of the East Midlands. Two of Dave's bands recorded at Beck in 1976 and again in 1981 and his experience was the same as everyone we spoke to when we began researching this book.

Many of the reminiscences in this book were taken from a Facebook page set up in Derek's memory a few years ago. Our thanks go out to everyone who posted and allowed us to use them in this account.

So, who was he? Derek's widow Mavis knew him the best. This is what she wrote:

'Derek was born in Rothwell on 1st December 1925. As a young lad he loved football and was a Patrol Leader in the Boy Scouts. He left school at 14 (top of class) at the outbreak of the Second World War.

Between 1941 and 42 he served with the local A.R.P. as a messenger, and from 1942 to 43 he served in the local Home Guard. According to his almost unreadable army records he was conscripted and sent to work down the coal mines as a Bevan Boy. He hated it and frequently went AWOL. According to Army records his mining career ended after he was 'Discharged through absence'.

He then enlisted into the Army. His REME (Royal Electrical and Mechanical Engineers) radar servicing record was very good, although I don't have much information personally. However, their remarks were: 'Intelligent boy, good scholar, quiet manner, speaks in a whisper (!), Slow to settle down but keen to please. Very good mechanical aptitude, main interest is wireless'.

During this time, he often came either on leave or AWOL from the mine to work for my father as a fitter at the Cytringan Welder Company.

I was sixteen at this time and was truly smitten with this tall, handsome Sinatra lookalike. We would play a riff or two of boogie woogie on my Dad's piano, and Derek became my chaperone on nights out at the pictures.

After discharge from REME in 1948 he lived with his mum in Laburnum Crescent, Kettering.

We began courting. I was working for my Dad and Derek had a job repairing TVs and radios at the Co-op furnishing department in Montagu Street.

By 1955 Derek was working for George Reader, who had a television and radio repair shop in Gordon Street. During this time, he made a crude radio receiver fixed in a vice in his bedroom in order to listen to the ham radio wavelengths. He could receive messages from my Dad aboard his boat the 'Cytringan'.

We married in 1957, and after living with Derek's Mum for six months moved into our first house in Belvedere Road.

Derek had been doing occasional work for my Dad and had kept up his interest in radio work but wanted to run his own electrical repair and retail shop. My Dad helped us out with the deposit, and we bought a former sweet shop in Regent Street a couple of years later.

We sold domestic appliances, but mainly televisions and Hi-Fi equipment. We were the main agents for top quality tape recorders like Grundig, Blaupunkt, and Telefunken.'

In the early 1950s Chris Barber's Jazz Band was one of the UK's busiest touring groups. They played trad jazz in clubs up and down the land. At one point during their performance the band's banjo player Lonnie Donegan played a selection of skiffle songs accompanied by double bass and washboard.

In July 1954 the Chris Barber Band went into the recording studio and Lonnie recorded two songs- 'Rock Island Line' and 'John Henry'. When they were released as a single in 1956, they created a nationwide craze for skiffle. Many well-known musicians including John Lennon, Paul McCartney, Jimmy Page, Hank Marvin and Bruce Welch began their careers by playing in skiffle groups.

Hank Marvin & Bruce Welch.

Mike Benford began his musical career as a member of The Keystones skiffle group. It was formed in the mid fifties at the Kettering Keystone Boy's Club. The club was originally housed in a disused pub in Rockingham Rd. The first line up was: Rod Derry on guitar & piano; Diz Leonard on guitar; Terry West (RIP) played tea chest/ double bass; Graham Sismey played washboard; and Mike on guitar and vocals.

They achieved some local fame when they passed an audition for the National Association of Boy's Clubs show at the Royal Festival Hall in London in 1956. They were rebooked for the following two years as well.

To add to the kudos of performing at the Festival Hall alongside the 'Forces Sweetheart' Vera Lynn, they were also invited to perform on the BBC's prime time pop show 'The Six-Five Special'.

The skiffle band morphed into a pop group when they bought an electric guitar. It was now the calypso era, so Graham and his washboard was replaced by Tom McEwan on bongos. He later procured enough odd drums and cymbals to make up a drum kit. In 1958 Phil Dainty joined on lead guitar. He was another future member of the Q-Men. The band came to an end in 1960 when Rod went to teacher training college, Tom went to Leicester Art College and Diz left to do his National Service in the army.

Mike Benford got to know Derek Tompkins through his shop in Regent Street. Derek sold him his first reel-to-reel tape recorder and got him hooked on high fidelity audio with brands such as Telefunken and Blaupunkt. Derek demonstrated to him that the current standard in Britain and the USA was very 'bass' biased. The continental brands showed the full range of sounds from rich full bass to crystal clear drums and cymbals. This viewpoint was to shape the future development of Derek's range of PA equipment.

John Dobson's 1955 British built EMI LS2 recorder. Derek used this machine to compare the quality with the German brands that he sold through the shop.

Telefunken Magnetophon 85.

Terry West, Graham Sismey, Tom McEwan, Rod Derry, Mike Benford, Diz Leonard.

Tom McEwan, Terry West, Rod Derry, Mike Benford, Diz Leonard.
The Keystones Skiffle Group.

Tean Green & the Drifters, about 1960.
Roger Thory, Dave Meeks, Les (Tean) Green, Barry Hart (hidden), Rob Thurland.

Roger Thory's first group was called Tean Green and The Drifters, formed in 1958/9.

All three guitarists (Roger Thory, Barry Hart and Rob Thurland) played through Rob's Vox amplifier. Roger played the bass parts on his Hofner Club 60 guitar before swapping it for a Hofner bass guitar.

After the demise of the Keystones, Mike Benford joined up with Roger Thory, drummer Jimmy Cameron and guitarist Barry Hart and formed The Teensville Four. They played a few successful gigs, but lack of transport and funds meant it was short- lived.

The Teensville Four. Left to right- Roger, Barry, Mike, & Jimmy.

The Corby Crows Nest youth club was set up by holiday camp owner Sir Billy Butlin in 1960. In March 1961 the Savoy Theatre in Kettering put on a 'Big Beat Night' in aid of the club featuring a host of local groups in a 'Battle of the Bands'. The organisers would have preferred it to have been held at the Corby Odeon, but the local cinema manager wanted nothing to do with it.

Adjudicators included artiste managers and promoters plus someone from the New Musical Express. Former Butlins Redcoat Ray Brett was the compere and Rock & Roller Vince Eager was the headline act, backed by the Ray Brett Combo. The acts included The Sapphires from Rushden; The Intruders from Peterborough, Corby bands The Strangers, The Crusaders, The Size Seven, and the Crazy Tones. Mike Benford sang 'Mystery Girl' backed by Ray Brett's solo guitar. The wording on the poster suggests that it was soon after the Teensville 4's demise.

Journalist Alex Gorden was on hand to record the proceedings-

'After receiving a terrific reception, Rushden group The Sapphires opened the show with Johnny Burnette's 'You're Sixteen', a young Barry Noble very much to the fore. Corby's Crusaders followed and gave a scintillating performance with their own arrangement of Donegan's 'John Henry' before completing the set with a rousing 'Yes Sir That's My Baby' and their tour de force, 'Glasgow Belongs To Me Cha Cha'.

All the bands performed to the best of their ability but in the end the Crusaders were crowned the Battle of the Bands Champions. The Size Seven's Brian Dowell and Alice Riley were proclaimed best male and female vocalists.

CHAPTER 3 - THE BIRTH OF THE Q MEN

In her book 'Making the Best of It', Mavis recounts that the Teensville's drummer Jimmy Cameron couldn't pay his TV repair bill so Derek took his drums as payment and set about learning how to play them.

In 1960/61 the hit parade was dominated by good looking teenage boys who appealed not only to the teenage girls who bought their records but also to the 'gay mafia' who controlled large parts of the music industry. It seems incongruous for a married man in his mid thirties to take up drums and start a pop group.

But that's just what Derek did.

(In 1961 Dave was 12. Cliff Richard was 22 and Derek was 36- two years older than Dave's father- DC)

We drew on the memories of the surviving band members to piece together the next part of the story, so the exact timeline cannot be determined. Roger Thory remembers that after the Teensville Four split up Barry Hart was contacted by Derek who wanted to start a band. Roger joined on bass.

He thinks that Mike Benford was in the original line-up but it's more likely to have been Mavis' brother John Dobson. His girlfriend Sue Garlick was their featured female vocalist. They called themselves the Barry Hart Quartet and played at a lot of different venues including US bases at Mildenhall, Alconbury and Chicksands. They travelled to the bookings in Derek's Bedford van. Derek later recalled-

'My first contact with music was when I had a hi-fi shop. Someone (Jimmy Cameron) owed a bill and offered his drum set in lieu.

I spent months in our living room banging away to music played on a tape recorder. Getting fed up with that I decided to join a group. After I was told that I was too old I formed my own.'

These photos are from Mavis' scrapbook. She thinks the first two were taken at the Alumasc Social Club in Burton Latimer in 1960/1. The picture on the right shows John Dobson with pre-Beatles hairstyle and playing his Guyatone electric guitar, the same as in the BHQ publicity photograph.

In the third picture John is wearing a gold lamé jacket. When the Barry Hart Quartet decided to adopt the same uniform, he was already kitted out.

Over the next few years Derek used his electronic knowledge to build a range of musical amplification gizmos, including mixers, amplifiers, speaker cabinets, and complete PA systems. The first of these was a bass amplifier. Roger Thory wrote-

'I don't know exactly when Derek started building amps, but I suspect that the one he built for me might have been the first. It was a 50-watt bass amp (powerful for those days). It wasn't the standard shape.

It had twin speakers and was taller than it was wide. It didn't have rounded corners and wasn't branded. When I left the group to go into the army in November 1961 it stayed with Derek.'

Derek's Bedford van outside the Regent Street shop. Early 1960s.

Roger's place was taken by Derek and Mavis' friend from their motorcycle club days, Roger Seddon. He played the bass parts on his Selmer Clavioline keyboard, introduced in the early 1950s and a forerunner of the synthesiser. It was the instrument featured on the Tornados worldwide hit 'Telstar'.

They wore made-to-measure matching gold lamé jackets and had publicity photos taken, but it soon became clear that something was missing- a bass guitarist.

In the autumn of 1961 Mike Benford was contacted by Derek and Barry Hart and asked if he was interested in joining their group. They were looking for an experienced male vocalist. At first, he resisted but agreed to go to a rehearsal to see how they shaped up. He said:

'I first met the group at one of their rehearsals in the North Park W.M. Club. There was Derek on drums, Barry on lead guitar, John Dobson on rhythm, Roger Seddon on Clavioline, Sue Garlick singer and another guy, whose name I think was Ron, also a singer. I had been asked by Derek to come and 'a-a-a-ave a listen', to see if I was interested in joining them.

First impressions weren't that favourable, but I saw that they were eager to improve and entertain. They just needed some grooming and slight changes. I thought about it and about a week later decided to join and the Barry Hart Quartet was ready to roll.'

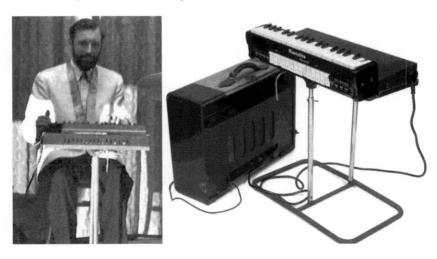

Roger Seddon and his Selmer Clavioline.

So, what did Derek have that would persuade prospective musicians to join him?

He had his own drum kit. He owned shop premises where the band could rehearse. He owned a van. Derek used the shop's buying power to purchase their equipment, including a mixer and six Reslo RBT/L ribbon type microphones which were so fragile that if you dropped one the ribbon unit broke and had to be replaced. (Mavis still has a number of replacement units.) They also had a Telefunken spring reverb unit that was so sensitive it had to be suspended on rubber bands.

Over the next few years, the Barry Hart Quartet became one of the best local bands. They were in great demand all over the county and out into East Anglia, playing venues ranging from military bases, WMCs, night clubs, colleges, and private functions like Hunt Balls and executive parties.

In February 1962 the film 'Twist Around the Clock' came to the Savoy cinema in Russell Street. The manager put on a Twist Dance competition and asked the BHQ to provide the music every evening from Monday to Friday, with the final on Saturday. There were two versions of the advert in the paper. The first advert refers to 'The Barry Hart Quartette'. By the time the film opened the billing had changed to 'The Barry Hart Quartette starring Mick Benford'.

Mavis has some photographs of the competition that were taken during the week. Three of the photos are reproduced below. Sue Garlick is in two of the photos. She is wearing different outfits. The bass player next to John in the bottom picture is yet to be identified. Was he called in at short notice to deputise or was he being auditioned? It's noticeable that the musicians aren't wearing their gold jackets.

During the spring of 1962 Barry left to audition for a professional job with Ray McVay's Band of the Day. His place was taken by Phil Dainty (previously with The Keystone Skiffle Group). However, after a week or two Barry returned to reclaim his place in the group and Phil left. Back in 2016 Barry wrote this on the Facebook page- 'I did a two-week trial and failed miserably. I'm not good in strict tempo or music reading situations. I could probably do better these days now that I've had my eyes fixed!'

Ray McVay had started out as a saxophone player in the big band era. His career took off when he became Musical Director for the Rock & Roll impresario Larry Parnes, manager of many pop stars including Tommy Steele; Billy Fury; Marty Wilde, Vince Eager and Joe Brown.

McVay led the band that backed the acts on the many package tours that crisscrossed the country, including the Eddie Cochran/Gene Vincent tour that ended in tragedy when their car crashed near Bath on April 17th, 1960, killing Cochran.

McVay was supposed to travel in the same car but there was no room, as Eddie Cochran needed to take his Gretsch guitar amplifier back to the US for repairs. Ray relinquished his seat and travelled in the van with the other musicians and equipment. That close escape from tragedy put an end to that stage of his career.

Soon afterwards Eric Morley booked him to work in his Mecca chain of ballrooms.

Ray set up his own dance band and worked in Glasgow, Edinburgh and Hammersmith Palais in London, before taking a long-term residency at Mecca's top venue, the Lyceum Ballroom in the Strand.

His band was also featured on the BBC's 'Come Dancing' programme for many years.

Barry had wanted to turn professional, but the others weren't in favour. Roger Seddon's business interests were taking up more and more of his time and he eventually put in his notice. Mike remembers that the members of the group had other commitments, families, and/or jobs, so their musical repertoire was restricted to covering the latest hits, with mid-week rehearsals and week-end gigs.

Soon after this they changed their name, partly because the name had jazz and classical connotations. There was a famous group at that time called The Modern Jazz Quartet. Secondly- they were no longer a quartet, so they became Barry Hart and the Q Men.

In April 1962 Barry and Derek visited Phil Dainty to ask him to re-join the group on bass guitar. Phil agreed but didn't have the money to buy an instrument, so Derek built him a solid bass guitar and sprayed it a lurid pink colour. Phil played it through Roger Thory's old bass amplifier.

The Barry Hart Quartet were out playing most weekends. On March 24th, 1962 they supported another local band The Senators at the Gaiety Ballroom in Ramsey. They were still known as the Barry Hart Quartet. When they supported the Mark Allen Group the following August 1963 they were billed as Barry Hart & His Q-Men.

In August 1962 Barry's girlfriend went away on holiday with her family. Barry had wanted to go with her, but the band had a prior booking. Derek proposed a solution. They would play the gig and then drive to Norfolk to spend the Bank Holiday weekend by the seaside.

Back in the early 1960s the August Bank Holiday was held at the beginning of the month and Sunday August 5th, 1962 will go down in history as the day when Marilyn Monroe was found dead in her bed. Both Mike Benford and Mavis remembered the date of the weekend for that very reason.

They took several cars, loaded tents and camping gear and a tape recorder from the shop. They packed power inverters in order to run the amplifiers from the car batteries and set off. They ended up at Wells-next-the-Sea.

Derek's wiring diagram for connecting the amplifiers to the car battery.

What followed was according to Mavis, a drunken, fun weekend, full of madness, where they entertained anyone within earshot. Roger Thory was on leave from the army and joined in the fun on guitar and was late getting back to Catterick Barracks and subsequently put on a charge!

Another friend, Barry Kinnear taped the band on one of the shop's Telefunken tape recorders.

After the August trip out to the seaside the Q-Men settled down to honing their craft by rehearsing every week, keeping up to date with the latest hit records and playing every weekend.

Q Men weekend at Wells-next-the-Sea August 5th, 1962.

John and his girlfriend Sue left the group towards the end of 1962. Their replacements were two more ex-Keystones, guitarist Des (Diz) Leonard and guitarist/keyboard player Rod Derry. Des said that he was asked to join the Q Men because they had begun to add Beach Boys, Four Seasons and Hollies songs to their repertoire and needed someone to sing the high harmonies. He could play rhythm guitar and that added an extra element to the sound.

The group relied on many of Derek's contacts for bookings and Mavis looked after the diary. She was so enthusiastic about this that they once turned up for a gig a whole year in advance!

Barry Hart posted this on the Facebook page shortly before he died:

'I was still pretty much a kid when Derek came into our lives. For much of the sixties the Q Men were his main interest. He had two principles:

1) The band had to be better dressed than the audience. Every year the first gig fees went to buy new made-to-measure stage clothes.

2) If you can't hear the PA (no monitors in those days), then you are playing too damn loud. It was also a test bed for his recording and equipment building. I grew up with the Q Men and I learned a thing or two, but also had an immense amount of fun.'

Rest in Peace Barry.

Mike Benford remembers another night when the Q Men were supporting the Barron Knights at Newmarket.

It was to be a defining night in the Q men history. Derek became lifelong friends with the Barron Knights and went on to produce all their 1970s albums at his Beck Studio.

For some reason they used the Q Men's gear that night. Mike said:

'We had no idea that our kit sounded that good. Peanut played a guitar solo through my amplifier that boggled my mind, but the main thing that we brought away from the gig was that vocals and harmony were what we wanted to sell, and so the Q Men's sound was born.'

The Barry Hart Quartet 1961. Barry, John, Roger S, Derek.

The Q Men- Phil, Sue, Barry & John.

CHAPTER 4: 1963

1963 was an incredible year that began with the Big Freeze, the coldest winter since 1947. Northamptonshire was frozen solid for months.

The newspapers were dominated by the Profumo scandal with all its twists and turns. He had been the MP for Kettering during the Second War.

In March Dr Beeching published his infamous report on the future of the UK's railways.

The UK failed in its attempt to join the Common Market.

The Beatles phenomenon began with the release of 'Please Please Me' at the end of January. It rose to number 2 in the singles chart and by the end of the year the band had scored three more number ones that together topped the charts for 18 weeks.

Date	Title, Artist		Peak Pos	WoC	Wks No 1
23.01 1963	PLEASE PLEASE ME BEATLES	PARLOPHONE	02	18	00
24.04 1963	FROM ME TO YOU BEATLES	PARLOPHONE	01	21	07
04.09 1963	SHE LOVES YOU BEATLES	PARLOPHONE	01	33	06
11.12 1963	I WANT TO HOLD YOUR HAND BEATLES	PARLOPHONE	01	22	05

In August the ongoing Profumo scandal was knocked off the front pages when robbers got away with over £2.5 million in used banknotes after holding up a train near Tring in Buckinghamshire.

Derek's health was never great. His wartime service down the mines, his heavy smoking habit, and living in a damp and almost unheated house during the coldest winter for years all played havoc with his chest.

At the same time as Derek's health was deteriorating Mavis discovered she was pregnant. Daughter Lynda was born on 25th August 1963 after a long labour while Derek was out playing with the band.

In November the world was shocked when President Kennedy was assassinated in Dallas. It was one of those events where people can remember exactly where they were when they heard the news. Princess Diana's death in August 1997 was another.

Derek struggled on through the winter, but it was obvious that he was very ill. On 6th April 1964 Mavis, accompanied by her mum and 8-month-old Lynda took Derek to Rushden Sanatorium to start his treatment for TB.

He was allowed out to celebrate his daughter's first birthday in August 1964. Mavis was kept very busy with a newborn baby, keeping the shop open and visiting her husband every evening. While Derek was out of action the band used a number of local drummers including Mick York (who used Derek's Premier kit) and ex-Keystones drummer Tom McEwan. He moved to Denmark soon afterwards.

Phil's pink bass guitar went missing after a booking and Des Leonard built him a brand new one in the week before the next show.

Derek was discharged on September 2nd and once he was fit enough, he went back behind the drum kit.

The Q Men wanted to produce a demo tape to play to agents, so Mavis fitted up the workshop as a temporary studio by glueing egg boxes all over the walls and ceiling.

Derek used his homemade mixer and the band's Reslo mikes, plus two Revox tape recorders and a Leak amplifier for play back.

Within weeks other groups wanted to record their own demos. Guitarist Steve Fearn first met Derek sometime in 1964 when he and his Leicester based band crowded into the makeshift studio in the workshop at the rear of the shop in Regent Street.

It soon became clear that he had to find different premises to record the bands. For a start Derek and Mavis had a young child to consider, the workshop was cramped and used for repairing TVs during the day. Recording had to stop every ten minutes or so because the shop was on a bus route and whenever one passed by the shop windows rattled!

As mentioned before, Derek had been designing and making amplifiers and speaker cabinets for local groups. Steve Fearn was one of Derek's early customers and used his Shield amplification for many years. Derek also built and installed systems in social clubs both locally and further afield, including the brand-new concert hall at the Kettering Windmill Club.

THE OFFICIALS AND COMMITTEE OF THE

WINDMILL CLUB

WELCOME ALL OLD MEMBERS, NEW MEMBERS, ASSOCIATES AND THEIR MANY FRIENDS
TO THE

NEW CONCERT HALL DANCE

ON

SATURDAY, 19th DECEMBER

Many thanks for your support—we are now a very large club, but we do not intend to forget those who supported us when we were small

WE EXTEND TO ALL A VERY HAPPY HAPPY CHRISTMAS AND ALL BEST WISHES FOR 1965

CHAPTER 5: HIGH FIDELITY VOCALS

We've already touched on the reaction to the Q Men's live sound and the quality of the vocal reproduction. It might be worthwhile at this point to look at what was available to budding musicians of the late 1950s/ early 1960s and to examine why the Q Men's PA sounded better than the others.

At the birth of Rock & Roll the average guitar amplifier was no louder than the radiogram in the living room. Indeed, many players started off by plugging their instruments into the radio or gramophone and even used them on their earliest bookings. Mo Foster's excellent book '17½Watts' (published by Sanctuary Music Library in 2000) is an often-hilarious account of those early days. If you can get hold of a copy, it's well worth a read.

When Cliff Richard and the Drifters started playing one-nighters on the cinema circuit in the late 1950s Cliff sang through the house PA- whatever it was. Hank and Bruce played through tiny Selmer amplifiers. I doubt if they could be heard above the screams of Cliff's fans. When Vox amplification offered the new AC15 to the Shadows they liked the sound but asked if they could have an amp that was twice the size and so the iconic Vox AC30 was born. At that time, it retailed at over £90, a serious amount of money when you took home less than £10 a week. By comparison a Watkins Dominator amplifier was only £38/10/-.

By 1960 guitar amps were twice as powerful as they had been a couple of years earlier. The next step up was to a 50-watt model and then in the mid 60s Marshall introduced their 100-watt amplifier which drove a cabinet (or two if you could afford them) containing 4 x 12-inch speakers.

Within a decade the ten-watt amplifier had been replaced by one that was ten times more powerful. Another change had taken place. Guitarists wanted an amplifier that when overloaded, would distort in a musically pleasing way.

The powerful humbucking pickups of the Gibson Les Paul guitar were perfect to get 'that' sound, and the era of the 'Guitar Hero' had begun.

The early Chicago blues players were among the first to incorporate distortion by turning their small amplifiers up to maximum. Gibson introduced the Maestro Fuzz Tone in 1962. This was the pedal that Keith Richards used when the Rolling Stones recorded (I can't get no) Satisfaction in May 1965. A couple of years later the Wah Pedal was launched and became yet another part of the guitarist's armoury.

The poor old vocalist was left behind, rendered inaudible by the sound of the band in full flow. So why hadn't the vocal PA systems kept up with the times?

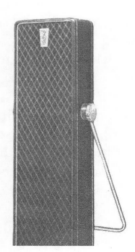

LINE SOURCE SPEAKER

This new scientifically developed model has been created with the same technical perfection that is associated with all VOX equipment. Having the advantages of giving a full spread of sound and minimising microphone feedback, this model is not only ideal for Public Address installations but is now fast becoming popular with the modern groups. Fitted with an adjustable stand which enables the Speaker to be set at any angle. Waterproof cover supplied. Incorporates four 10" Dia. Speakers, 40 Watts output per Cabinet. 15 ohms impedance Dimensions: 45½" high × 13" across × 7½" deep.

From the 1964 Vox brochure.

As previously mentioned, in the late 1950s the singer used whatever Public Address system was available. Very few had a PA of their own. He might plug his mike into a spare input of the guitar amplifier. Many bands started out that way with all the guitars and microphones sharing a single amplifier.

Those PA systems that were available were expensive. The speakers were tiny and had a limited frequency range. The manufacturers tried to overcome this by arranging multiple speakers in a tall narrow cabinet. The amplifiers had only the very basic tone controls and no more than four inputs. If turned up too loud the speakers were prone to feedback and the sound was distorted.

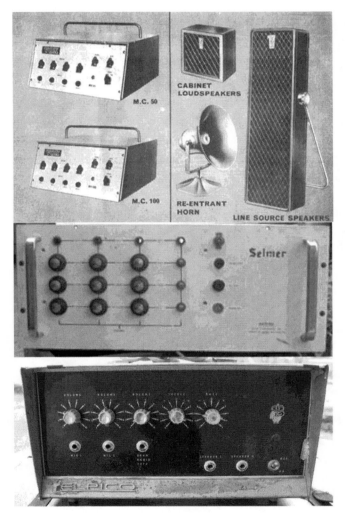

1964 PA amplifiers. Vox, Selmer, ElPico.

Derek's shop sold quality hi-fi systems. He preferred the German made tape recorders and hi-fi systems because they could accurately record the full spectrum of sound from low bass to the highest treble. It got him thinking about building what was essentially a scaled up hi-fi system for the vocal PA.

Sid Watkins of WEM (Watkins Electric Music) also thought along the same lines. He invented the slave amplifier system in the mid 60s. This is how it worked. Most amplifiers have two inputs per channel. You plug the output from the mixing desk into one of the inputs on the amplifier. You then plug a lead into the other input and connect it to the second amplifier, meaning that both are amplifying the same signal. BUT- this produces a loud mains hum through the speakers. Watkins got around this by removing the earth wire from the slave mains plug so that both amplifiers are earthed through the signal lead. You need more power? Add another slave amplifier (minus earth). This enabled the estimated quarter of a million plus people who attended in August the 1969 'Stones in the Park' free festival to hear clearly, using only a dozen or so standard PA systems slaved together.

Dave writes: I was there. I couldn't see the stage, but I could hear everything clearly. I'm told that the residents of Edgware, seven miles away could also hear!

700 watts of WEM power slaved together.

Derek was well on the way to designing and building the best PA system on the market. He had the electronics skill and experience from working on radar installations in the late 1940s and repairing TVs and other electrical goods at his shop in Regent Street. He was also an experienced metal worker and welder from his time working for Mavis' father at the Cambridge Street factory. He had access to the best audio systems on the market and he was a gigging musician. He knew what he wanted and set about designing and building it.

In the meantime, he continued making amplifiers and speakers for clubs and groups, including some for Roger Thory's army band in 1965. Roger had been posted to Nairobi for a couple of years and later when he was posted to Germany, he decided to form a group. Roger wrote this:

'In 1965, I set up a group with other lads in the Regiment. We had instruments but no amps. The C.O. authorised a loan from Regimental funds.

We bought 2 x Linear 50-watt amps and had Derek make us speaker cabs consisting of two guitar cabs and two P.A. columns. They can be seen in the photos on Pages 42 & 43.'

The PA amplifiers on the market were utilitarian metal boxes with only the most basic features and more suited to installation in a club or factory. They had a maximum of four channels and only the most rudimentary tone controls.

The Q Men used six microphones, so Derek designed and built an amplifier with six channels, all with individual tone controls for treble and bass. An external echo/reverb unit could be connected by way of a 5-pin din socket and each channel's level of echo could be individually controlled.

Derek hand wired and soldered every component. Mavis also had a hand in the manufacturing process when she cast all the front panel knobs from a special plastic material. They used red Dymo tape for the front panel channel markings.

Derek used a top of the range Leak amplifier for the power stage and the completed unit was mounted in a wooden case covered with black rexine styled cloth. The early models were unbranded.

The major manufacturers were using cheap all-purpose 8- or 10-inch loudspeakers, and Derek's first cabinets were the same.

He then designed a speaker cabinet that used top quality Goodmans 12-inch speakers and tweeters- a scaled up hi-fi speaker cabinet. When coupled to his new PA amplifier the results were outstanding. Every local band wanted one. Derek was kept busy hand wiring and assembling them in the Regent St shop before going into business with Mavis' brother John and taking over his father in law's old factory in Cambridge Street in 1966. Mavis's younger brother Alan also helped in the factory.

Roger Thory's army band 1964/5. Derek built the PA speakers.

Gibson SG guitar, Linear 50-watt amplifier and Derek's 2x12 speaker cabinet.
Roger Thory looks pleased with himself!

In 1963 Dave Wagg was living in Wellingborough and playing drums for a local band called The Fireflies. They often played in Kettering and one Sunday night in around 1965 met up with the Q Men at a band show at the Granada cinema.

Dave remembers this very tall lanky man playing drums who had a permanent smile and a pleasant drumming technique. The other bands included The Invaders with Mu Duncan and Formula Five from Corby. He said:

'I could not believe the vocal sounds coming from singer Mick Harper of the Formula Five and wanted to know how this was achieved.

Step forward Derek Tompkins at the end of the show. 'Yyyyyou need a good sound system. I can build you one, come and see me at my shop in Regent Street.'

Some weeks later, off we go to meet Derek and young Mavis at Derek's shop. Talk about Aladdin's Cave, there was electrical stuff everywhere, switches, dials, cables, plugs and other assorted hardware the likes of which I had no idea what it was, did, or how it worked. Several visits later and after more tea from the lovely Mavis, Derek had built a system that gave us that sound we had been looking for.'

Dave Clemo: I was still living in London in the early 70s but had a gig at the US Air Force Alconbury Officers Mess with an Irish band. All our kit was primitive to say the least, but the headline band had a Shield PA and sounded great. It wasn't until I moved to Northampton in 1974 that I discovered who made them.

Peter Grantham's Shield PA amplifier.

CHAPTER 6: THE WINDMILL CLUB 1965

When Kettering's Windmill Club's concert hall was officially opened in December 1964 the double page spread in the local paper included an advert for Derek's PA systems.

Note that the advert says, 'sound reinforcement' and not 'amplification'. There's a subtle difference between making a sound audible and making it louder. It's a way of describing quality of sound as opposed to quantity. This club's target audience had lived through the wartime. They didn't like loud noises. They wanted a quality sound. Baby boomers were different. We wanted it LOUD.

When Derek supplied the club's new PA system, he offered to maintain it in exchange for the use of the main hall stage on Sunday mornings to record groups. He still had to record the vocals back at the shop. It wasn't suitable for the long term but was a step towards setting up a dedicated recording studio.

Derek had a good ear for music. His experience as a drummer in one of the top local bands and an almost forensic ear for sound frequency and tunefulness soon had the local and not so local musicians and singers beating a path to his door, including Ray and Ann Brett, an up and coming duo from Corby.

Ray grew up in Bedfordshire where he first learned to play guitar. He had his first professional job in 1959 as a Butlins Redcoat. After the season ended, he took up a new post with another Billy Butlin sponsored project at the Crows Nest youth club in Corby. He met and married a singer named Ann and they began to work together professionally.

Ray is a talented songwriter and, in the spring of 1965, decided to record one of his songs at Derek's. The session took place one Sunday morning at the Windmill Club.

His musicians for the session were Dave Anderson on drums; (Dave later switched to banjo, guitar and pedal steel guitar and became a stalwart of the British country music scene.) Jack Thomas played bass and seventeen-year-old Nick Evans was on lead guitar. It was Nick's first ever recording session.

First of all, the instrumental track was recorded. Once that was 'in the can' it was time for the backing vocals to be added. Derek blended the vocals and instruments and recorded them via a second tape recorder. In order to take advantage of the natural echo in the corridor outside the hall, Nick, Jack and Dave donned headphones and stood around the microphone while the backing track was played, moving close or away from the microphone as required.

Derek could hear their footsteps in his headphones, so he told them to take their shoes off and tiptoe! Ann and Ray finished the record back at the shop and as already mentioned their session was interrupted every time a bus went past.

Nick Evans and Dave spend an entertaining couple of hours with Ray and Ann while researching the book and towards the end of the afternoon Ray revealed that he still had the recording and had converted it to an MP3. The song was 'She's Sweet'.

Ray played the song to us. The look on Nick's face was a picture. This was the first time he'd heard the track since he helped record it over half a century earlier.

Ann & Ray Brett.

The Kettering Advertiser printed this article written by Linda Hutchins in their edition dated Friday May 13th, 1966:

'A husband and wife team whose voices span the age groups.'

'Few performers have the ability to appeal to all age groups, although it is obvious that the wider range of appeal an artist has the better.

Basic pop artistes have been quick to appreciate this fact and their fans span the age groups, but they are few and far between. I can think of Elvis Presley, the Beatles, Freddie and the Dreamers, Joe Brown and the Walker Brothers, possibly Dusty Springfield, but not many more off hand.

Corby's Ray Brett and Ann have this ability.

I can think back to a few years ago when Ray was a wild young rocker, fingering chords on his electric guitar with bewildering speed and chanting beat songs like 'Lovey Dovey' and 'Good Rockin' Tonight' when he was resident singer at the Crow's Nest Club. It is hard to believe that it is the same young man who walks on to a stage these days neatly togged out in dark suit, frilly shirt, and bow tie and quietly strumming an acoustic Spanish type guitar. Ray sings with his golden-voiced young wife Ann now, and their popularity is sweeping through the East Midlands club circuit like wildfire. The accent in their music is on melody and harmony, but occasionally Ray still likes to let rip and Ann will join him in a vibrating duo-voiced beater like Ray's self written 'She's sweet'.

Basically, Ray and Ann's music is Country and Western coated lightly with a sparkling sprinkle of pure pop. The end result is good, solid entertainment with the same ageless appeal that made the music of Jim Reeves so popular.

I doubt if Ray would like to return to those old days of being the teenager's idol. Now he is an entertainer.

And I'm sure that he and Ann are destined to go on to even greater fame and probably fortune.'

Barry Fletcher first met Derek when his band (an early version of The Minor Portions) recorded at the Windmill in 1965. All the vocals had to be recorded back at the shop. He later joined Barbary Coast who achieved international fame as Frank Ifield's backing group. More about him in Part 2 of our story.

The Fireflies were another band which Derek recorded at the Windmill Club. The session was featured in an article by Linda Hutchins from the Northants Advertiser of July 1966.

'Cutting a Demo' with the Fireflies.

In a small back street off one of Kettering's main roads, lurks a tiny radio shop. Cluttered with equipment, and usually cluttered with people, it would be difficult to believe that it is the Mecca of most local pop groups.

The shop is owned by Mr Derek Tompkins- himself a drummer in a local group- a dedicated perfectionist who is responsible for putting most of the successful local talent on the right road.

He uses the equipment he has made and adapted to produce demonstration discs for the groups to take to recording sessions. And he charges them only the cost of the tape to make the recordings.

One group, which has taken advantage of the facilities just recently are the Wellingborough Fireflies, who produced a 'demo' of the Gidian recording 'Fight For Your Love' a couple of weeks ago.

Making such a recording is a hard and seemingly unprofitable task. The group learned the song and went along to the Windmill Club in Kettering at eleven o'clock one Sunday morning to record the backing.

There are six members of the group and each instrument had to be perfectly co-ordinated to get the right effect.

The leader is 18-year-old lead guitarist Mick Cox, who is still at school in Wellingborough. His father is the manager of the group and the one who spurs them on.

Then there are brothers David and Derek Wagg. David aged 23 is the drummer and twenty-year-old Derek is the singer. Saxophonist John Tyrell aspires to be a poet at the age of 17, while bass-guitarist, Ben Jenner (23) is a butcher.

Eleven o'clock on a Sunday morning isn't exactly the best time of the day to appreciate the poundings and excessive amplification of this young and versatile group, but when I arrived, they had made a trial recording, and were listening to it to make adjustments.

Each instrumentalist had a microphone and Derek had to adjust the pitch and sound to balance the music.

Derek feels that the group has a lot of promise. They are enthusiastic about their music and not primarily interested in making money: 'Although', they told me, 'A hit record wouldn't come amiss.'

In a number like 'Fight For Your Love' the arrangement was there, and they could adjust it for themselves.

During the morning they kept repeating the same music over and over again.

'The organ isn't right'...

'The sax is too loud'...

'That wasn't a bad recording, but it sounded empty in places.'

Four hours later, after a few cross words, the backing was ready and all that was needed was the vocal on top of it.

The demo tape is made in two parts and then put together afterwards.

'The backing and vocal are never exactly synchronised on the same tape' Derek told me, 'and this is the reason why we use two.'

The groups all use the Windmill Club because the acoustics serve the purpose adequately.

In the afternoon, they had to practice for a show at the Granada Cinema, Kettering, and then it was back to the demo disc.

Singer Derek Wagg, who had been practising all morning but not over-working himself was in for a hard job.

The group went back to Derek Tompkins shop, and singer Derek was put in solitary confinement with a pair of headphones, to add the vocal to the backing.

He said he wasn't very nervous, but his hand was shaking as he listened to the music piped through to him and he began to sing.

It didn't help with the other members of the group asking him what happened to his voice, but he got through and the trial disc was complete.

Once the disc has been made the group will be able to take it to a professional recording studio and show them how they want their music arranging.

With a professional studio they have to play against time, and they haven't always got the time and patience to perfect a disc, and this is why many of the groups fail to come up to scratch when they go for a recording audition.

They are not prepared for what is to come, and it doesn't help.

Are the efforts of Derek Tompkins to go unnoticed forever? Gidian, the successful Corby singer, made his first demo disc there, and so did Barry Noble from Isham. The Invaders- with Little Mu got two recording tests from demo discs made there.

Derek hasn't any (Brian) Epstein type ambitions, he maintains he does it for a hobby, and is only interested in seeing local groups get on in the proverbial world of pop. But he deserves much of the credit for their success and gets little.'

(More about The Fireflies on page 116.)

This may have been the show referred to in the article.

Linda's observation about the record company's studio time being at a premium was proved correct time and time again as several groups and artists discovered to their cost when the record that was supposed to break them into the big time was inferior to the demo that they made with Derek, as we shall see in later chapters.

The unintended consequence of this free publicity was that even more bands and singers wanted to record with Derek, and it was becoming clear that the Windmill was no longer suitable.

During 1966 Mavis' father sold his business and the old factory building in Cambridge Street was empty. Her brother John could see the possibilities of using the old factory as a base for building Derek's increasingly popular amplification range, while Derek could envisage how part of the factory could be converted into a recording studio. The stage was set.

Mu Duncan & The Invaders pose for the camera in 1964. Bass player Roger Buckby appears to have lost a string on his Burns guitar. He is standing in front of what looks like one of Derek's hand-built cabinets. The guitarist next to him is future Pesky Gee and Black Widow member Kip Trevor.

Adverts from 1963. Dale Viccars was singer Derek Wagg's stage name.

One Nighters at the Granada 1964.

Kettering was on the Granada cinema circuit.

Mike Benford left the band in around 1965. Des Leonard took over as lead vocalist. He had about three weeks to learn the words to thirty or so songs in their repertoire. He admits that for the first few gigs the songs had some strange lyrics, but it all added to the fun. When Des left in 1971 Mike rejoined in his place.

Very little is known about the bands that John Dobson played in after he left the Q-Men at the end of 1962. Mavis' diary records that he played with a group called The Tabbycats at a dance at Sywell on 22nd Feb 1963.

The following year he was rehearsing with The Detours, playing his new Hofner Galaxy guitar. In April 1965 the band won a competition in Northampton and got their picture in the local paper.

The Detours, a Kettering group, are the only local unit to reach the finals of the Midlands Top Ten Group contest.
They got through the semi-final at the Plaza Cinema, Northampton, on Sunday,
when there were some high-class performances.

CHAPTER 7: 1966

1966 was another memorable year for music. During January The Beatles' double 'A' side single 'Day Tripper/ We Can Work It Out' continued its run at number one, followed soon after by 'Keep On Running' by the Spencer Davis Group.

Roger was at college in Chelsea and has photos as well as posters from the time SDG played at his college on Saturday February 6th, 1966, the day they toppled the Beatles from Number 1. (Derek would later play a big part in the recording career of their drummer Pete York).

The Barron Knights scored a top ten hit with 'Merry Gentle Pops' and went on to record at Derek's Beck Studio throughout the 1970s. Derek's friendship with the group had begun a few years earlier when The Q Men supported them in Newmarket as recounted earlier.

That summer the Crows Nest in Corby organised one of the first open air concerts.

CORBY'S FIRST OPEN AIR BEAT CONCERT

Pop fans crowded around the Civic Centre, Corby, on Saturday afternoon when the first open air beat concert was held. Different groups played on a bandstand beneath the council chamber.

The Beatles continued to dominate the charts and their album 'Revolver' set the standard for other studios and groups to aspire to. The Beach Boys had four consecutive top ten hits and spawned a host of groups who copied their sound, including groups like Deuce Coupe and The Endevers, both of whom played in Kettering regularly.

Don Maxwell posted this on the Facebook page a couple of years ago:

'Music was moving on very quickly in the mid 60's and I was playing bass with the Endevers.

I can remember seeing Formula Five and listening to the best vocal PA sound we had ever heard. We learnt that it was a Shield system and incorporated the first use of tweeters that I had seen.

It had been built by Derek and within a week or two we had bought our own. We were at that time very much into Four Seasons/ Beach Boys, and with our new Shield PA were suddenly one of the best vocal harmony bands around, and all thanks to Derek.'

Don't talk about problems when you meet The Endevers, a Hitchin (Herts.) based group who've been taken under the kindly wing of Nems and who make their disc bow with "Remember When We Were Young" for Decca. This group, which has come together from all over the country, have experienced such trials as having their gear stolen, running out of money at the most difficult times, and sundry other troubles. However, their own good humour, which stems from their lead guitarist, Des Anderson, Fife-born and a guiding light in their affairs, looks like carrying them through.

The Endevers 1968.

The Endevers recorded at Shield before being signed to Decca in 1968. Don later became a part of the trio Canned Rock. They finished second behind comedian Jim Davidson in a national TV talent show and in the late 1970s were one of the best live bands in the UK.

Dave remembers seeing them play live and their version of Queen's Bohemian Rhapsody was absolutely note perfect, including the semi operatic part in the middle where their three voices sounded awesome.

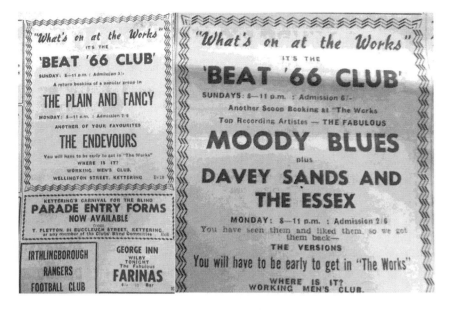

Kettering Working Men's Club was the top venue in 1966.

July and August 1966 were notable for several landmark events. The second Cambridge Folk Festival took place over the weekend of the 9th and 10th of July. The first one was held in 1964 and over 50 years later Cambridge Folk Festival still ranks as one of the best, and one of the few that continues to use the same venue.

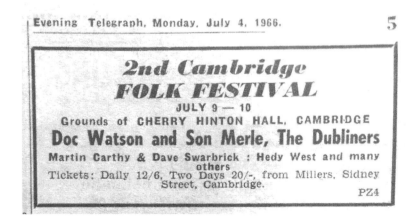

61

The government passed the Marine Offences Act into Law on July 28th; on the 30th England won the World Cup, and Cream made their first festival appearance on the 31st.

Front page news.

The Sixth National Jazz and Blues Festival took place on Windsor Racecourse over the weekend of the 29th-31st of July 1966.

Festivals were often used as debuts for upcoming acts and this weekend was notable as being the first major UK debut of Cream on the Sunday night, the band having only played one other warm-up show in Manchester a couple of days earlier. At the time the advertising bills and posters were printed they had yet to decide on a name so were listed individually. As is all too common it rained during their set and the festival turned into something of a mud bath, but it did not dampen the enthusiasm of the crowd.

The first headline show for Clapton, Bruce and Baker. Contrary to other accounts
Cream never played the Tin Hat in Kettering.

The Beatles released their groundbreaking album 'Revolver' on the 7th of August 1966.

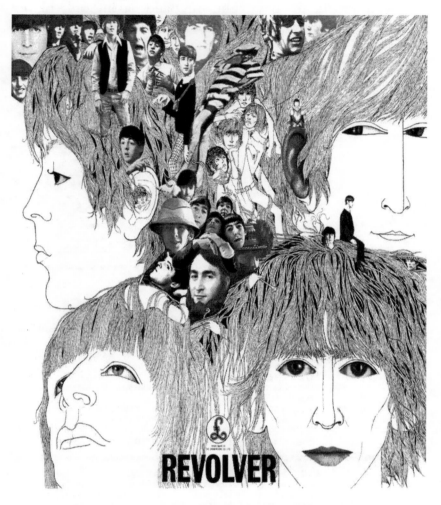

Klaus Voormann's Grammy award winning album artwork.

CHAPTER 8: IN THE NEWS

By 1966 the Q-Men were arguably the best semi pro group in the area, playing clubs, society parties and Young Farmers balls. They had a full diary, playing most weekends while holding down full-time jobs.

The Northants Advertiser of July 1966 published this article, as usual written by Linda Hutchins:

The Q Men play it cool.

'Ten years ago, the hot pop scene saw a promising Kettering skiffle group leap to fame on the with-it programme '6-5 Special'.

The group was known as 'The Keystone Boys' and they brought the Donegan touch to the outback.

Where are they today? Enjoying the fruits of the big-time, living in a luxury villa in Southern Italy, sailing a yacht in the Indian Ocean? No- the original members of the group are settled down happily in their hometown, enjoying the enjoyment of the people who listen to them at local parties and private dances.

The original boys, Mike Benford, Tom McEwan, Rod Derry and Diz Leonard promised to follow in the footsteps of the Johnny Duncan and the Blue Grass Boys and other popular house-shakers. They appeared on television and Phil Dainty joined them when they played the Festival Hall pop concerts in 1957 and 58.

Then Tom, Mike and Rod went to college. Diz joined the Army, and Phil went to Kettering Technical College. So that finished all their dreams of stardom.

Some years later a young man named Derek Tompkins, who owned his own radio shop in Kettering desperately wanted to learn to play the drums.

He applied to most of the groups for someone with the knowledge, patience and ear drums to teach him, but he told me, 'they all thought I was so bad nobody would teach me.

The only answer was to form my own group.'

To do this he enlisted the aid of a successful young guitarist- Barry Hart- who had just left another group. Together they went around to all the members of the 'Keystone Boys' and they formed 'The Barry Hart Quartet' - later to be known as Barry Hart and the Q-Men.

Their first *(major)* booking was playing with the Chubby Checker film 'Let's Twist Again' at the Savoy Cinema Kettering, and they went on from strength to strength and they became the top group in the district.

The Q Men in Derek's workshop.
Back- Derek & Rod; Middle- Phil, Mike & Barry; Front- Des.

But stardom doesn't shine out of their eyes. They are not interested in the big time with their name blazoned across the metropolis in big lights. They insist that they play for a hobby.

'We've kept the bookings down to two a week.' Derek told me. 'We all have homes and wives to think of and we all have our jobs.'

Rod is a schoolteacher, Phil a foreman at a local shoe factory, Mike the assistant manager of a shoe factory, Barry a shop manager and Derek has his own shop.

They've had plenty of offers to go abroad and turn professional, but the life doesn't appeal to them one little bit.

'We're just not wild enough and we are content just to play as a hobby' they said.

Derek has used the group to experiment with the new equipment he builds- public address systems, amplifiers, reverberation systems. They have tried all the latest things and been the guinea pigs.

One of their proudest possessions, and their mascot, is the van which they travel to bookings in. The van has acted as their home when they have broken down and it has fallen to pieces.

'One night we were driving home from a booking at great speed when the door flew off', they recalled. On another occasion they attempted to mend a puncture and found that some considerate person had walked off with the spare wheel, so they found themselves laden like pack horses, hitching a lift back from Cambridge.

They play to varied audiences mostly the young people who grew up in the rock 'n roll era and who appreciate the sound they make.

Nowadays they do not fill out the local dance halls with the latest gimmick in the national charts. They play at private parties where the fans are not-quite-so-young.

For this they must be adaptable and claim to be able to play anything the audience requires, from Chopin to Lennon-McCartney compositions.

Their appeal is more than just the hip-swivelling foot-tapping moddies with the Vidal Sassoon haircuts and Mary Quant dresses. They cater for everyone- and cater very well indeed.'

Mike Benford said that Derek thought that setting up equipment on stage was too time consuming, so he built one huge cabinet to house the amplifiers. He built speaker cabinets using a variety of bass, mid range and tweeter speakers to create a hi-fi quality PA sound.

Nick Evans remembers seeing the Q Men one Sunday night at the Granada in Kettering. One of the amplifiers was playing up. Everybody in the venue must have heard Derek shout 'Kick it!' Mike Benford had a half-hearted attempt before Derek got up from his kit, his right trouser leg tucked into his sock to stop the bass drum pedal getting caught. He walked over to the cab and gave a well aimed and weighted kick that cured the crackle. That was the mark of a true professional. He knew exactly where- and how hard to kick it!

1963 dates.

1964 dates.

A few adverts for the band from 1966 & 1967.

CHAPTER 9: DEREK LEAVES THE Q-MEN

By the end of 1966 Derek's business was growing. He was busy repairing TVs at the shop. In addition, he was making amplifiers and speaker cabinets for local groups and clubs. He'd also set up a recording studio in part of the old factory in Cambridge Street.

To say he was kept busy was an understatement. Not only that, he had a wife and three-year-old daughter to consider. Something had to give.

In the spring of 1967, a further element was added to the mix when his brother Brian decided to open the old Tin Hat club on the corner of Rockingham Road and Britannia Road as a music venue. See Chapter 15 for more about the Tin Hat's history with Derek and Brian.

Brian Tompkins.

Derek reluctantly made his decision to leave the Q-Men. This advert appeared in the ET in June 1967:

It was followed a few days later by this article in the local paper:

Drummer to quit Q-Men

'Derek Tompkins, the daddy of the local drumming world has announced his intention of leaving the group the Q-Men as soon as a replacement can be found. Derek and his brother Brian have recently started a real discotheque snowball at the Tin Hat in Kettering.'

Derek's last show as the drummer with one of the region's top bands was probably when the Q-Men were the support act on the Grand Opening Night of the Tin Hat in June 1967.

Derek's replacement in the group was Keith Ward. We contacted him and he had this to say:

'I am the 'new man' who took over from Derek, but I may not be the best person to answer your questions. It all happened in a bit of a blur and now I remember less about those days.

Des (Leonard) tells me the audition was at his house in Rothwell. I don't know if they saw any or many other applicants. I seem to remember being told we had a booking, so I did my first gig with them without any practice session - a mixture of pure joy and sheer terror - it was a VERY good band.'

Derek continued to manage the group after he left, with Mavis looking after the diary.

SHIELD ELECTRONICS

D. S. TOMPKINS   J. R. DOBSON

CAMBRIDGE STREET
KETTERING

TELEPHONE 81591

P.A. SYSTEMS · CUSTOM-MADE AMPLIFIERS
LOUDSPEAKER ENCLOSURES   DISCOTHEQUE EQUIPMENT

Shield Electronics 1966-69.

Derek- drums; Phil- bass; Des- vocals; Mike- vocals, guitar; Rod- vocals, guitar, keyboard; Barry- lead guitar, vocals.

After Derek left the band.

Phil; Des; Rod; Keith Ward; Barri Michael Jones; Barry Hart.

CHAPTER 10: MAKING RECORDS

For the first half of the twentieth century making a record was exactly that. You sang or played, and your performance was recorded. The skill of the engineer lay in his ability to place the microphone(s) in the right place and ensure that the equipment functioned correctly. His aim was to capture the best possible performance in the shortest time with the fewest mistakes.

By the mid-sixties recording techniques had advanced to the point where it was possible to create music in the studio that couldn't be played live. Several contemporary composers like Stockhausen were starting to use tape loops in their compositions. Other studio effects included double tracked vocals, flanging, reverse drums and looping. *(Further explanation can be found at the end of this chapter.)*

Back in 1947, recording pioneer and genius Bill Putnam produced the first recording of a single vocalist harmonising with herself. The singer was Patti Page and the song was 'Confessing'. She recorded the harmony onto an acetate disc which was played back as she sang the main vocal line on to a second recording lathe. She went on to sell millions of records in the 1950s, including her most famous song 'Tennessee Waltz'.

Putnam was also responsible for inventing or introducing many of the features of the modern studio including multiband EQ, compressors and tape echo.

Audio recording comes a distant second when compared to the human ear. It cannot reproduce the full frequency range or difference in sound levels from very quiet to very loud that we take for granted. Putnam developed the compressor, a device that 'put a lid' on the loudness of the signal being picked up by the microphone without compromising its quality.

He also pioneered the use of electronic filters that made it possible to isolate and adjust the different frequencies in the audio spectrum.

It was then possible to boost or cut them and achieve a balanced sound, with nothing too loud or too quiet, and nothing too screechy or boomy, and all controllable by the turn of a knob or the flick of a switch.

Les Paul took things to a whole new level in 1947 when he discovered that if he slowed the recorder to half speed and recorded a part, it would sound an octave higher when replayed at normal speed. Les Paul's recordings of 'Lover (when you're near me)' and 'Brazil' featured eight different parts on electric guitar including several recorded at half speed. They were recorded straight to acetate, one part at a time. The next track was recorded by playing back the first acetate and recording the second guitar on to another disc. The two tracks were then played back while Les recorded the third part, and so on. He used over 500 blank acetates before he was satisfied with the end result.

Les Paul's 1948 album was recorded using acetate discs. A few years later he worked with Ross Snyder of Ampex on the world's first eight-track recording machine.

In 1949 Bing Crosby gave Les Paul a brand new Ampex tape recorder and the rest, as they say, is history. The records he made with his wife Mary Ford still sound amazing today.

At first, he used a single machine fitted with an extra record head, but there was a potential problem.

Recording one track on top of another using a single machine meant that mistakes couldn't be corrected, and you had to start again. Eventually Les got around this by using two identical machines and built up the tracks by 'bouncing' them from one machine to the other, like this: Record one guitar on machine A, then record the second guitar and the track from machine A onto machine B. Then play back machine B and record the third part together back on machine A and so on.

Back in the 1950s and early 1960s the secret of getting a good recording was to arrange the musicians around the microphone(s) so the loudest instruments were further away and didn't drown out the quieter ones. Rudimentary tone controls enabled the engineer to control the treble and bass.

Les Paul's recording experiments led to Ampex introducing the first 8 track tape recorder in 1956. (See the picture on page 75.) It used eight recording heads stacked one on top of each other and recorded on to a one-inch wide tape. Each track could be individually adjusted or muted and overdubbing was possible. Different parts could be recorded without affecting the other tracks and each channel could be individually adjusted to achieve a perfect balance. Studios still continued to record in mono using 3 track machines and it was to be another decade before they came into common use in the US, with the UK studios following a few years later. Eventually it was normal for studios to use 16 or 24 track machines recording on to two-inch-wide tape. Towards the end of the 1970s some studios linked two machines to provide 48 tracks.

The first British song that Dave can recall which featured double tracked vocals was 'Bobby's Girl' by Susan Maughan. It was a hit over Christmas 1962 and was pop perfection to his ears.

The Beatles 1966 album 'Revolver' is a landmark in many ways. The Beatles and their producer George Martin made a deliberate decision to create the tracks using everything the recording studio had to offer. Twenty-one-year-old engineer Geoff Emerick and technical manager Ken Townsend were responsible for getting everything down on tape.

Dave Clemo clearly remembers the first time he heard the track 'Tomorrow Never Knows' and thinking that he'd never heard anything like it. He hadn't. Nobody had. It was truly ground-breaking.

In the 50s and 60s most records were recorded in mono. Very few households owned a stereogram. Stereo records were few and far between. The stereo mix of a song was usually done as an afterthought. There's a famous story about John Lennon playing a stereo mix of 'Sergeant Pepper' to a friend. When he commented favourably Lennon is reported as saying 'You should hear it in mono!'

At the other extreme, the stereo 'mix' of Frank Ifield's 1962 hit 'I Remember You' was nothing more than the backing track in the left channel and his solo vocal in the right.

All this technical innovation was expensive. Very few London studios had the equipment, resources or engineering expertise of Abbey Road and demand pushed the price beyond the reach of the songwriter looking to make a demo that he could play to a publisher or A&R man. There was an opening in the market for studios that offered a quality product at a reasonable price.

When Derek opened Shield Recording Studio in 1966, he was well placed to meet this demand.

It may be worth while at this point in the story to include a brief explanation of some of the studio jargon. In the days before automated mixing and computer programming became the norm, everything had to be done by hand.

The studio engineer's skill lay in using whatever tools were available to create the sound that the producer and artiste were looking for.

So, let's start with reverberation, or reverb for short. We all know what it sounds like. The sound of your voice strikes hard surfaces like walls, ceilings and furniture and is reflected back to your ears a tiny fraction of a second later. It is used to great effect to fatten up the sound of a singer or instrumentation. Churches and theatres are designed to make the best use of the effect. Anyone who has sung in a dead, reverb free room or in the open air will know (by its absence) the benefit of having a little reverb to help you.

It is not the same as an echo, when a word or piece of music is repeated back to you after you have sung, spoken or played it. The first echo or reverb chambers were simply an enclosed space with a loudspeaker at one end and a microphone at the other. The amount of reverb or delay could be adjusted simply by moving the microphone closer or further away from the sound source. Guitarist Duane Eddy's trademark 'twang' was created by playing a recording of the sound of his guitar bouncing around in an empty oil tank, recording it and mixing the reverb signal with the original. The drawback was that the studio was located next to a railway track and recording had to be stopped whenever a train passed by. Derek had a similar situation when recording at Regent Street. Whenever a bus went by the shop windows rattled!

Dusty Springfield recorded her vocals in the stairwell outside the studio. The natural reverb was perfect for her voice. When Derek began recording at the Windmill, he used the natural reverb in the corridor to record the backing vocals.

But what if it wasn't possible to use a convenient space to record? Several mechanical/electrical devices were invented to try and replicate the sound. The first was the spring reverb unit, patented by Laurens Hammond in 1939 and fitted to his Hammond organs. Instead of using a large empty space the signal was fed down a long spring causing it to vibrate before being picked up at the other end.

This was the same system employed in the Q Men's Telefunken reverb unit and shared the same drawback. Any stray vibrations (for example- rocking the unit back and forth) set off a thundering crashing sound. However, their small size lent them to being incorporated into guitar amplifiers.

The next development took place in 1957 with the introduction of the EMT Reverb Plate. A sheet of metal was suspended on springs in an enclosed space. The signal was fed into one end of the plate, causing it to vibrate. An adjustable transducer picked up the signal and fed it back to the mixer desk where it was blended with the original signal to create the desired effect. It was about 8 feet x 4 feet in size and weighed just over a quarter of a ton. It was incredibly expensive (one could buy a house for the same amount of money), so Derek built his own.

Les Paul's experiments with tape echo in the early 1950s led to Charlie Watkins' invention and introduction of the Watkins Copicat in the late 1950s. Charlie got the idea for a tape echo machine after hearing the effect in a studio, where several professional tape recorders had been hooked up to produce multiple repeat echoes. Watkins thought it would be a pretty neat trick if he could reproduce the effect in a single, portable box – and with the use of three tape-record and playback heads, he did just that.

A single loop of tape, driven by a motor, passed over the record heads, giving three preset tape-delay times, selectable by means of three push-buttons. The first gave a very fast slap-back-style echo; the other settings gave longer repeat times. Once the tape had passed over the record heads the sound was erased by magnets.

The Binson Echorec used a revolving magnetic drum instead of tape and its most famous users included Shadows guitarist Hank Marvin in the 1960s and Pink Floyd's David Gilmour in the 1970s. Derek had been given a Binson Echorec by the Barron Knights and used it in his studio while he was developing his plate reverb.

From the 1950s composers and studio engineers turned their attention to the tape that was used to record the sound. What if that could be manipulated to create different sounds? Flanging was the first. Les Paul (him again) released a record called 'Mammie's Boogie' in 1952. He recorded it on acetate discs rather than tape, but the flanging effect can clearly be heard.

In 1959 Toni Fisher recorded 'The Big Hurt' at Gold Star Studios in Hollywood.

The producer thought her vocals sounded a bit thin, so he re-recorded it onto a second machine. There was a slight speed differential between the machines, so he held his hand on the flange of the reel to try to keep the speed constant.

The result was a 'swoosh' or 'jet plane' sweeping effect. It was so new and captivating that the studio released it without any further changes. It was the first record to feature the flanging effect and was a big hit, reaching number 3 in the US Billboard chart and peaking at number 30 in the UK. The engineer on the session was Larry Levine who went on to help Phil Spector create his 'Wall of Sound' a couple of years later.

This classic effect was further developed by Abbey Road engineer Ken Townsend in the spring of 1966. John Lennon was tired of the laborious process of recording dual vocal tracks and asked Townsend if there was some way for the Beatles to get the sound of double-tracked vocals without doing the work. Townsend devised artificial double tracking or ADT. George Martin credited Lennon for naming the technique 'flanging'. It was only available in the larger studios but within a few years every record was overloaded with it. Another closely related effect was phasing which was achieved by passing the signal through filters and mixing it back into the original signal.

A further development involved the use of stopwatches, razor blades and splicing tape. A music loop is a section of a piece of music or sounds edited in such a way that it can be seamlessly repeated. Loops can range from a few seconds to many minutes in length. Sometimes the tape was reversed and fed through the recorder, so it played backwards. One of the best-known examples is the ending of 'Strawberry Fields Forever' by the Beatles, recorded at Abbey Road in November 1966.

The engineer of this session was 21-year-old Geoff Emerick. He also suggested running Lennon's vocal through a Leslie rotary speaker cabinet (normally used with Hammond organs) on 'Tomorrow Never Knows'.

He then blended the recording with the original to produce the effect.

Geoff was also responsible for the circus/fairground sounds on 'Being For The Benefit Of Mr Kite' on Sergeant Pepper. Producer George Martin suggested that he cut the tapes with a pair of scissors, throw them up in the air and splice them together at random. (From Mark Lewisohn's book 'The Beatles Recording Sessions', published in 1988).

Derek was a regular visitor to Abbey Road Studio from 1967 onwards and would have seen these developments at close hand. No doubt it fired his imagination at what could be achieved, even with his more basic studio set up.

Abbey Road Studio 2 1966. EMI REDD.37 desk and Studer J37 recorder.

CHAPTER 11: RECORDING AT SHIELD
(Part 1)

Derek's use of the Windmill Club stage on Sunday mornings lasted about a year. It all changed in early 1966. The demand for his recording expertise was growing, so much so that he set up a studio in a spare room at the Cambridge Street factory.

Derek wrote this:

'My father in law had a business that manufactured electric welders, and when he sold up the factory in his backyard became vacant. I had been building amplifiers and loudspeakers for bands and I suggested that his son and I could use it to start a business. One part of the premises was not used, and I turned it into a small studio.'

He continued to design and build PA and disco equipment under the Shield label, assisted by Mavis' brothers Alan and John, who also worked on the sales side.

Brian Tompkins, Alan Dobson and their Shield disco equipment.

Over at the Nags Head in Wollaston 'Big Bob' Knight had recently started a disco night that proved very popular. He used a twin turntable disco deck that had been imported from Japan.

Derek looked at it and within a few weeks had designed and marketed a twin deck disco unit under the Shield label, using two Garrard SP25 turntables.

It was a success from the outset and almost every local DJ used them. He introduced a matching amplifier at the same time. Brian's mobile disco was advertised as the 'Tompkins Sound' and was a perfect advert for the brand.

The studio's customer base expanded from being mainly local groups in the Kettering/Corby area to acts based in Leicester and beyond.

Many were local bands who wanted to make a record to keep as a souvenir, while some had their eye on a recording contract with a major label.

One such hopeful was seventeen-year-old Trevor Horn from Leicester. In 1966 he was playing bass for Steve Fearn's Brass Foundry and was looking for a local studio to record a demo tape. Steve recommended Derek so he made the trip down to Kettering to record a demo that featured him singing, playing piano and bass guitar.

He paid close attention to how Derek used his two Revox machines to double track various parts and learned as much as he could about the recording process.

About ten years later he was able to set up his own studio in Leicester before finding fame with his group Buggles ('Video killed the radio star').

He got more acclaim as a record producer responsible for Dollar, ABC, and Frankie Goes to Hollywood's chart successes in the eighties. He was a co-founder of the electronic group Art of Noise and his production of Seal's 'Kiss From A Rose' in 1994 earned him a Grammy to go with his three Brit Awards from 1983, 1985 and 1992.

In 2010, he received an Ivor Novello Award for Outstanding Contribution to British Music. He was a major influence on pop and electronic music in the 1980s:

And it all began with Derek Tompkins at Shield.

There was also a demand from songwriters, both local and further afield, for reasonably priced studios to record their compositions to play to music publishers in London.

All the equipment in the studio had been hand made or adapted by Derek and there are many recollections of him disappearing under his desk to make some running repair. Steve Fearn remembers visiting him in his workshop. He said 'Derek never used to switch anything off and was getting electric shocks all the time. He'd go straight into the amp. You could see it flashing. He was completely immune to electric shocks. He'd had so many that they didn't have any effect.'

Another feature of his studio was the cigarette burns on many of the surfaces. Derek was a heavy smoker and very often he left his cigarette to burn down to the butt while he busied himself on something or other.

Derek wrote these notes a few years before he died:

'I started my recording studio with six individually boxed microphone amps feeding into a home built six channels by two out mixer which was intended to be the prototype for a new amplifier range that we were going to introduce.

This fed to two Revox tape recorders, I also needed a decent reverberation unit, so I made a steel frame in which I fixed a 4ft x 3ft rolled steel sheet on which were mounted home-made drivers and accelerometers. After thousands of hours of experimentation, it proved so successful that it stayed in use for the whole period of the studio.'

(Driver= speaker. Accelerometer = pickup.)

The unit was loosely based on the EMT Reverb Plate that had been introduced in the late 1950s. There were a couple of differences- one being the size of the unit and the other being the price. The EMT was very expensive. That may have been the reason why Derek spent countless hours developing his.

Former Endevors and Canned Rock bass player Don Maxwell remembers Derek showing him the new reverb unit that was kept in an outhouse at Shield. He said it was his pride and joy. Roger Thory also remembers seeing it in the workshop a couple of years earlier.

Darren Harte is a radio presenter, record collector and vintage vinyl trader and is the BBC local radio's go-to person when discussing all things vinyl. He says that Shield and Beck recordings have a distinct sound that is hard to describe but is instantly recognisable once you know what to listen for. This is almost certainly down to Derek's reverb unit.

In the 1960s and early 70s every studio had its own 'sound'. Discs recorded at Abbey Road sounded different from those recorded at Regent Sound or in Joe Meek's studio above a shop at 304 Holloway Road. This distinctiveness was lost in the mid-to-late seventies when studios were designed to sound exactly the same. Many hit albums were recorded using different studios in different cities and occasionally in different countries. It was therefore advantageous for the studios to sound the same, but something was lost along the way. When someone says that today's songs all sound the same, it's because the studios are designed that way.

The first domestic tape machines recorded at $3\frac{3}{4}$ inches per second. Any fluctuations in the voltage could result in the machine speeding up or slowing down, known in the trade as 'wow and flutter'. The effects can be mitigated by recording at a faster speed. Derek's machines were set to run at 15 inches per second. Other machines ran at 30 inches per second.

He continued to use the Revox machines after he moved the studio to Wellingborough. In 1971 he uprated to a British built 8-track machine before getting a convertible Scully tape recorder that could be run either as an 8-track or uprated to 16 tracks.

When Derek first started recording groups at The Windmill, he would present the finished product to the artist on a reel of mono tape.

Derek Wagg, Tich Edson & Fearns Brass Foundry recorded this demo for Robin (Tracy) Goodfellow. The acetate was cut at Advision.

Acetate discs had to be ordered from Advision in London. He realised that if he had his own lathe, he could cut discs so his customers could quickly hear how the session went. On December 6th, 1968 Derek paid £150 (a significant sum) for a second-hand disc cutting lathe from a studio in Cambridge.

He had identified another gap in the market. As well as cutting acetates for studio users Mavis remembers that Derek copied acetates for Northern Soul Disc Jockeys. They used to queue outside the shop in Regent Street and came from miles around. It paid for itself in less than a year.

The lathe was installed in the Regent Street shop. As you may know, the sound of a vinyl record is reproduced by a diamond tipped stylus travelling along a groove.

John Tompkins took this picture of Derek's Scully disc lathe.

The stylus converted the vibrations into an electrical signal that could be amplified. Derek used the lathe to cut the groove. It was a highly skilled operation but well within his capabilities. The discs were copied in real time, meaning that a 3-minute-long record took three minutes to cut (plus setting up time.) No wonder there was always a queue.

Shield and Beck acetates are getting scarce. Every now and then a very rare gem surfaces and causes excitement among record collectors.

CHAPTER 12: THE CANADIANS

In October 1966, seven young Canadian musicians arrived in England determined to make their mark on the British music scene. Their drummer Barry Casson had spent six weeks in London and believed that the band could succeed there. They'd already had some success in their native Victoria, British Columbia where they were known as Bobby Faulds and the Strangers. They felt that they'd gone as far as they could and needed to break out. They recruited teenage keyboard player David Foster who had recently been a member of Ronnie Hawkins' Hawks, before setting off overland from Vancouver to Gander in Newfoundland where they picked up their flight to London.

The Canadians presented this signed photograph to Derek & Mavis.

The full line-up was drummer Barry Casson, a brass section consisting of Rich England and Wes Chambers on saxophones and Bill Stewart on trumpet and trombone, organist Dave Foster, bass guitarist Mike Stymest and their vocalist/guitarist Bobby Faulds who had recently changed his name to Bobby Hanna.

Bobby had relatives in Kettering, so they decided to base themselves there rather than in London.

News of their arrival spread fast and they were befriended by Derek and Mavis who arranged for them to stay at the Sun Hotel in Market Street. It was pretty run down and cold, so Mavis organised electric blankets and took the band under her wing. They used Derek's studio in Cambridge Street as a rehearsal room and settled down to make contacts in the UK music business.

The band got an agent and starting touring. They changed their name to the Canadian Strangers before becoming The Canadians. They began by playing some local shows and soon teamed up with Corby based singer Gidian (aka Jimmy Pollock). He had recently moved down to London and had been signed by a major agency.

Journalist Linda Hutchins wrote several articles about the group for the local press, including this one from The Kettering Advertiser in October 1966:

'Canadian Strangers make their debut.'

'If you're bursting with curiosity to see the new Canadian band who have teamed up with Corby's Gidian, now's your chance, for they'll be making their debut at the George Inn, Wilby, on Sunday.

The seven young Canadians- known as the Canadian Strangers- are ambitious and confident and provide a worthy backing for the talented Gidian.

The boys left their jobs on the off-chance and came to this country in a bid for success. You judge their potential for yourselves, but I think they have great possibilities.

The appearance comes just after the release of Gidian's new record 'Feeling', which came out yesterday. Self penned, the record has a big band backing- by the Canadians- and a very impressive beat, and it could be the badly-needed break for Gidian.'

Another article by Linda followed a couple of weeks later:

'Don't write off Canada's pop yet.'

'Can't you get your weather fixed?'- the opening gambit from the Canadians, whom I found swathed in thick overcoats huddled together in Kettering's Shield recording studios waiting to practice.

They've been in Kettering just over a month and they are still complaining about the cold weather! But they're very warm hearted and agreed they hope to stay in the country to make a go of their kind of music.

One thing which has impressed them since they came to this frozen isle is the advanced state of music:

'In Canada they're still raving about the Stones and the Beatles, but the kids here like a different type of music,' they told me.

'But we've found the music that we're doing is going down very well, kids here enjoy it and appreciate it which makes it a lot easier for us.'

The boys are determined to start at the bottom and work their way up, and so far, they've found nothing but roses.

At the moment the idea is to build up a package show featuring the Canadians, Bobby Hanna, and Gidian, and with a collection of talent like that they can be a tremendous success.

Their music is fine, but their biggest problem is accommodation. No-one seems to want to rent a house to seven of the nicest Canadian imports since highly polished pine.

Competent they might be, dynamic they might be, but this doesn't give them the sense of being 'all-conquering'. They practice religiously every day to perfect their music, to keep up to date with all the latest sounds, and to make sure complacency doesn't drive them out of the running.

They love Britain and I feel they have great potential here. Judging by their former success, they will have no difficulty at all in putting Kettering on the pop map- even if they are Canadian.'

This is from Barry Casson's website:

'We left Victoria wearing nice blazers with a Canadian Maple Leaf Crest on our jackets. At the time that's what we thought was cool, maybe for here but for England? Wrong!

Our first gig at Leicester University was playing on a stage at one end of a huge gym. Another band used the stage at the other end. They were 'The Move' who went on to become 'The Electric Light Orchestra'. We played our set and then they played theirs.

We wore our tight white legging pants, boots and a kind of buckskin shirt with leather laces in the collar. We thought this would be a cool outfit to wear on stage. Wrong!

To be honest we had never seen anything like this. At the perfect moment, our lead singer Bobby turned to us and said, 'Let's do the Tony Bennett ballad 'I Left My Heart in San Francisco'.

That comment broke the ice and we laughed like crazy as we realized we were totally out of our element at this gig.

We did go on to do some Motown hits which saved our butts and got us through the evening with a reserved response. We were simply not prepared for that British scene at the time'

(More at barrycasson.com)

They began working with Corby based singer Gidian. Linda Hutchins posted this review of their first show in the Kettering Advertiser dated Friday November 18th, 1966.

Most exciting package show.

'Take seven maple-leafer Canadians and a pint sized Gidian and you have one of the most exciting package shows in modern pop history.

When they appeared at the Granada, Kettering on Sunday they took the audience by storm, shattering the usual feeling of apathy which comes after a late Sunday lunch, and sending all-Canadian boy excitement bouncing from the gods.

The show opened with an instrumental number from the Canadians which prepared the audience for the dynamic duo to come.

Then their vocalist, Bobby Hanna, appeared with the same tinselly sparkle in his eyes, and the same impish grin and bounced into a Tom Jones number.

His finest performance, without a doubt, was of the croony ballad 'Hey Girl' when Bobby came down into the audience. It was a shame it was marred by the man on the spotlight who spent some time flashing round the auditorium trying to find the elusive Mr Hanna.

When Gidian arrived on the scene complete with his new disc 'Feeling', which is placed in the Radio London top twenty, it was too much for a handful of girls in the middle, who let out embarrassed screams each time he twitched a hip or shook a finger.'

Barry Casson described when the band played The Cavern Club in Liverpool on the 18th December 1966:

'We started getting good press in the Melody Maker. From the good press we were getting, our agent got us booked into the Cavern in Liverpool. It was a huge thrill setting up on the stage where it all started for the Beatles. The Cavern was literally that. Red brick arches with a low ceiling that had a claustrophobic feel but was great for atmosphere. Our big brass sound filled up the place and our reviews from the gig were top notch.'

From the Kettering Advertiser December 1966:

Contract for Canadians

'With a hop, skip and a jump the Canadians have landed firmly on their feet and have signed a contract with London agent Roy Tempest for a series of tours and possible recording rights.

The contract is over a six-month probationary period with an option for three years.

What of Corby's Gidian who was being featured with the group? 'We made a couple more records backing him' said Barry, 'but the rest is up to our manager.'

So, it doesn't look as if we'll be seeing much more of the 'why- don't- you- get- your weather- fixed' Canadians in this part of the country. The contract includes a five-bedroomed flat- 'Well we need that many bedrooms with seven of us'- and a new van.'

Mr Tempest is wasting no time. The Canadians will make their first appearance at the Oasis Club Manchester on Sunday, and then from there they will begin a ten-day tour with America's Drifters.

They have two more tours arranged before Christmas and January 25 they begin touring with Billy Stewart- and not just as a backing group.

The Canadians will be blazened all over the posters- featuring vocalist Bobby Hanna.'

Alas, all was not well. Barry wrote on his website:

'The three horn players were all married and had to convince their wives that we could all do this within a few months. Unfortunately, they could only send home so much money each month and this created a crisis when all three members had to leave and return home. Boy did we ever miss their sound. We were now down to me on drums; David Foster on keyboard, Mike Stymest on bass along with our singer Bobby Hanna.'

The band posing for the photographer. Shield Studio, Feb 1967.

The Kettering Advertiser February 17th, 1967:

Canadians return

'Remember the Canadians- Kettering's foster group of lovable imports who left for London and a career in the big-time some two months ago?

Well they were back in Kettering last week making a re-recording of their latest single with Derek Tompkins at the Shield recording studios.

The boys have very depleted forces since they first waved goodbye to the green grass of Kettering and said hello to the Smoke.

Three of them have returned to Canada, leaving only singer Bobby Hanna, guitarist Mike Stymest, drummer Barry Casson and organist Dave Foster to keep the maple-leaf flag flying in this country.

The new record has been written by Bobby and Dave and has a tremendous vocal rhythmic mixture which could easily put them where they belong.

The lyrics are refreshingly original, if not a little significant, and tell of a stranger's feeling in large London town without a friend.

Could this have been written from the heart? Whether it was or not it's a great sound, and with luck should be released in the coming month.'

Barry recalls what happened next:

'Our agent was bringing over American acts as they were huge in England at the time and he felt that we knew their sound better than the Brits, and so we were booked as Chuck Berry's band for his British tour along with gigs in France.

He was a big star in Britain at the time and many of our gigs had major security and some riots along with police and guard dogs. It was all very exciting to be Chuck's drummer. We played big ballrooms and Universities always doing Chucks' mega hits like 'Johnny B. Good', 'Roll over Beethoven' and 'Sweet Little Sixteen'. He was a Rock n Roll Legend, even back then.'

January 1967's gigs included a tour backing The Drifters, while February was taken up with the Chuck Berry tour and the visit to Shield studio. In March they backed Inez & Charlie Foxx and in April they played dates backing Bo Diddley.

In late April/early May Bobby Hanna left the group to go solo, and the Canadians finally folded in June 1967.

David Foster played in the Warren Davies Monday Band for a couple more months before returning to Canada and embarking on a hugely successful career as a record producer, winning scores of awards and composing many million selling records. While he was based in Kettering he spent as much time as he could at Shield studio with Derek, learning everything he could about the art and science of recording. Derek taught him everything he knew, and David never forgot that.

Chuck Berry and the Canadians 1967. (Barry Casson's photo).

The Warren Davis Monday Band. David Foster 3rd from left.

When his stint with the Warren Davis band came to an end David returned to Canada. In 1971 he joined the pop group Skylark. They signed with Capitol Records and released an album that spawned a US top ten single 'Wildflower'.

After the band disbanded Foster remained in Los Angeles. He was a session player on George Harrison's album Extra Texture in 1975. A year later he played his Fender Rhodes and clavinet on George's album Thirty-Three & 1/3.

In 1979 Foster was a major contributor to Earth, Wind and Fire's best-selling album 'I Am'. He co-wrote six of the tracks including the worldwide hit 'After the Love Has Gone', which won the 1980 Grammy Award for best R&B song.

Since then the list of artists that he has worked with reads like a 'Who's Who' of the best selling late 20th century music business, from Whitney Houston, Celine Dion and Michael Jackson to Diana Krall, Dolly Parton and Michael Bublé.

Foster has won 16 Grammy Awards, including three for Producer of the Year, an Emmy Award, and a Golden Globe. He has also been nominated three times for 'Best Original Song' at the Oscars.

And it all began with Derek Tompkins at Shield.

David Foster evolved from a 12-year-long bout with classical piano into a respected rock arranger and composer.
At sixteen, David toured Europe as a sideman for Chuck Berry and Bo Diddley.
Then it was back to Canada, where he acquired a fine reputation as a writer ananger.
David is responsible for the choice arrangements and co-production of the music that is Skylark.

Northants Advertiser Friday June 2 1967.
Teenscene by Linda Hutchins.

Bobby Hanna of Canadians goes solo.

'Bobby Hanna strolled into the office with Isham model Barry Noble on Saturday and announced that he and the Canadians parted company after a recent trip to Cologne.

The group went down (to London) nine months ago when Roy Tempest took over as their manager. The three members of the brass section returned to Canada at the end of last year, while Barry Casson, Mike Stymest, Dave Foster and Bobby remained.

They played in clubs dance halls and cabaret all over the country and then last month toured Cologne.

'We had a wonderful time even though it was very hard work with seven or eight shows a night,' Bob told me.

'The weather was great, the food, beer and girls were great. In fact, everything was fabulous, but we still missed England.'

When they returned, the boys had serious discussions about their future, and each decided he wanted to go his own way in the pop music business.

So they split up and drummer Barry Casson is now preparing to take a year's drumming tuition and working in cabaret at night.

Guitarist Mike Stymest and organist-arranger Dave Foster have teamed up with a new drummer and another guitarist to make an 'under 20' group.

They hope to be working for Starlight artists- the agency which brings groups to the Works, although they are not expecting to be launched for another month.

And Bob? Well you may have heard his new disc on pirate radio- an appealing Les Vandyke composition 'Thanks to You.'

He's now being managed by Maurice Press, husband of Eve Taylor who manages Sandie Shaw and Adam Faith.

Any records discarded by Gene Pitney and Engelbert Humperdinck are passed over to Bob who hopes to record one next week for release on Decca in July.

'My last disc sold about 1,000 and the company were very pleased with it,' he said.

It was plugged on all the commercial stations- a climber on Caroline- and for a first disc that can't be bad.

Ultimately Bob would like to do cabaret.

At present he is sharing a Kensington flat with Barry who is still thriving on ads and cabaret. Barry has a permanent two-night booking as a fill in for artistes on 'Top of the Pops' and is recording again in the next few weeks.' Linda Hutchins.

Evening Telegraph,
Thursday, May 1, 1969.

BALLAD FROM HANNA

BOBBY HANNA is a young Canadian who made several appearances in this area when he first arrived in this country a couple of years ago.

Since then Bobby has made quite a name for himself and could have his first big hit with a new Decca release called "Winter Love". It is a big Italian ballad given a strong send-off by Bobby's rich and mellow voice with some ear-catching swirling and crashing strings.

If on Decca listen out

Gidian (Jimmy Pollock)'s wedding to Elizabeth Plaistere
at Hammersmith Registry Office on 24th June 1967.
David Foster was his best man and Mike Stymest was a guest.

CHAPTER 13: BARRY NOBLE

Barry Noble is undoubtedly one of the most successful singers from this area. His musical career began in the late fifties when he played guitar in a skiffle group called The Skiff-Rocks. They used to practise in the cellar of his father's pub The Red Lion in Isham, just outside Kettering.

In those far off days before groups were amplified if you wanted your band to be louder you added another guitarist. The Keystones had three guitarists as did The Double Diamonds from Market Harborough featuring a young Steve Fearn. One day Barry was asked if he'd like to join The Sapphires and after passing the audition, he became their third vocalist and rhythm guitarist.

By 1960 they had switched to Hofner guitars and Selmer Truvoice amplifiers and were gigging around the clubs and US Airbases in the East of England. One night they supported Neil Christian and the Crusaders who featured 16-year-old Jimmy Page on guitar. The Crusaders made a great sound as a quartet and within a few days the Sapphires had slimmed down to a four piece with Barry as lead vocalist. Barry stopped playing guitar to concentrate on his singing.

The Sapphires in 1961.
Barry with Chris Frost- guitar; Bruce Smith- drums; Johnny Keys- bass.

During the early 1960s they often supported bands like Emile Ford and The Checkmates, Johnny Kidd and The Pirates and Cliff Bennett and The Rebel Rousers. In 1961 they took part in the Battle of the Bands at the Savoy and played a couple of dates at the Gaiety Ballroom in Ramsey; the first was in July when they were supported by a local band called The Marvins. *Did they play Shadows tunes?* In October the Sapphires were back at the Gaiety and played all night without a supporting band.

September 1963   October 1963

November 1963   December 1963

In June 1964 they were back at the Gaiety this time supporting Brian Poole and The Tremeloes. Later that year they played a show in Wellingborough.

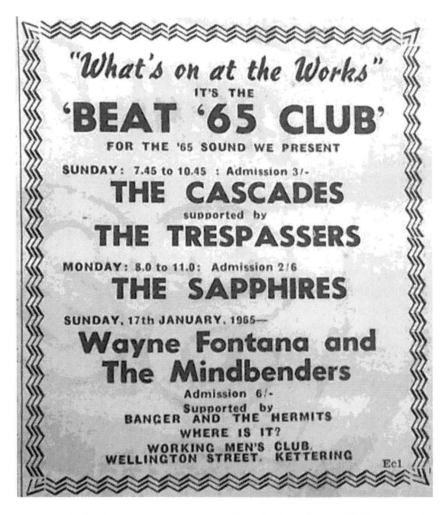

Barry left the group to go solo during late 1965 or early 1966. One Sunday he recorded a demo at The Windmill Club. The Evening Telegraph's Graham Faulkner wrote this article early in 1966-

Local singer looks set for stardom

'Seven years after forming his own four-man pop group, Barry Noble, the twenty-one-year-old singer from Isham, has been given the chance of turning professional and breaking into the national pop scene, writes Graham Forrester.

He has signed a management deal with John Newman, of John Mason Artistes Management, and Howard and Blaikley who manage The Honeycombs.

So impressed are they with Barry's potential that they hope to have a record released for him by March.

'It certainly looks like being Barry's year' said John Newman, who spent a year looking for the right singer before he signed Barry.

Ken Howard and Alan Blaikley have written three songs for Barry which he has already rehearsed. 'They are just great; they are brilliant song writers' said Barry.

Confidently John Newman told us 'I watched Barry and decided he had a terrific potential. Frankly I am so confident of Barry that I feel this year will be very successful for him.'

Another big move to launch Barry to stardom has been the formation of a fan club. It is felt this will also serve to bring together his already numerous fans.

The fan club needs a secretary. 'If there is any girl who would like to take on the job, she should contact Barry at his home, The Red Lion, Isham' said Mr Newman.

A year after forming his own group Barry joined the Sapphires. It has been with this group that he has already made a name for himself. Billed as Barry Noble and the Sapphires he has travelled up and down the country giving performances.

He joined the Sapphires as a rhythm guitarist and worked his way to become the group's vocalist. Before joining them, he was with another local group, The Vigilantes.

Said Barry, 'I was introduced to John Newman at a party and he came down and heard us at a booking and was kind of knocked out. He wondered what I had been doing'.

After this Barry passed a couple of television auditions but was unable to appear on any shows as he had no record released.

'John came along at the right time. I was getting really depressed,' continued Barry.

With his managers he feels that he is really suited to ballad singing, and although he can play the guitar, he prefers to remain solely a vocalist.

After supporting most of the top attractions in the pop business Barry certainly knows what it is all about.

One claim to fame so far is that he was voted 'Britain's Undiscovered Boy Friend of 1963' in a national magazine competition. Then he was offered recording opportunities, but nothing came of them.'

From the ET in 1966.

Despite the confidence displayed by his managers it was hard to get his singing career going. His first record didn't come out until 1968 and gigs were few and far between. A friend introduced him to a modelling agency, and he got some well-paid work making TV commercials and the odd walk on parts on television.

In September 1966 Linda Hutchins wrote this article for the Northants Advertiser:

'Sing-swinging advert model, Barry Noble, is going great guns with his career. Since July he has appeared in a number of walk-on television parts. In 'Adam Adamant' arrayed in full evening dress, he danced with a young girl, and in a 'Twenty-four Hours' skit, he played- don't tell me you didn't recognise him in that helmet- a policeman.

With numerous film-parts behind him including 'The Jokers'- a sequel to 'You Must Be Joking' and the new Dudley Moore film, Barry is now trying to concentrate a little more on his singing career.

He had a very successful cabaret booking at the sophisticated 'Greys Club' in Liverpool and hopes to go for a week's booking in Manchester next week.

It is in the wind that there may be a contract for him to sing for a certain well-known pop group manager- but as I said that is in the wind.'

Teenpage by Linda Hutchins. April 28th, 1967.

1967 is promising year for Barry

'To hold your own in show business these days you must be versatile- any real professional will tell you that- and Isham's Barry Noble is no exception.

1967 has found this young model-cum-singer-cum TV actor in a veritable whirl of versatility.

Barry has made appearances in TV shows ranging from 'Dr Who' to the 'Newcomers' and from 'Top of the Pops' to a 'Learn Spanish' programme.

'I was a tourist in the Spanish show, a waiter in The Forsyte Saga, a monster called a Cyberman in Dr Who, a guard in a new 'Three Musketeers' series and a policeman in a recent Wednesday play' he told me in a letter. 'I stood in for Georgie Fame and Vince Hill on 'Top of the Pops' and have had small parts in 'The Troubleshooters' and 'Honey Lane'.

But versatility in television isn't enough for this energetic young man who now shares a flat with The Canadians in London's Gloucester Road.

In the modelling world Barry has been working as the handsome he-man in the Big Fry ad for the Sunday Times as well as bobbing about for Cherry B and advertising Benson and Hedges cigarettes for the national newspapers.

If you happened to see 'Georgy Girl' when it came to local cinemas you may have recognised Barry's voice singing one of the songs.

'My mother went to see it and she enjoyed it very much' he wrote. 'She said she dragged my relations along to see it as well!'

At present Barry is waiting for his manager to return from the States before going into the recording studio to make his new disc.

'We have recorded several really good songs', wrote Barry. 'They're hard to find these days.'

This year promises to be very fruitful for Barry. We wish him the best of luck in every field he's exploring, and look forward to see him soon, whether he's disguised as a robot in Dr Who or whether filming adverts....'

Linda Hutchins wrote this article for the Evening Telegraph of Feb 28ᵗʰ, 1968:

10 Evening Telegraph.   Wednesday, Feb. 28, 1968.

From television adverts to the top of the charts?

From television adverts to the top of the charts?

Barry Noble, the Burton Latimer pop singer under contract with Nems Enterprises- the agency which launched the Beatles on the road to fame- has cut his first single disc.

One of the first artists to be signed to the recently formed MCA record label, his first single entitled 'I Can't Forget' will be released on March 8th.

Written by Don Black, the song was the winning number at the Yugoslav Song Festival last autumn. This is the latest success for 25-year-old Barry, who spent several years on the production side of the shoe trade before entering the professional pop world. At 14 he was singing in local functions and later he joined local group 'The Sapphires' as lead singer. He remained with the group for about four years.

About four years ago a girl friend submitted Barry's photograph to a teenage magazine and much to his surprise he found himself tagged 'Boyfriend of the Year', which earned him a night out at the magazine's expense.

In February 1965 Barry decided to try his luck in London, but work was difficult to come by except for a few cabaret dates in Wales and the north of England.

To help with the money problem a friend introduced him to the Peter Benison Agency and Barry discovered that the modelling business paid quite nicely. This led to TV commercials.

At that time, he started being offered small parts on television and in films, hence the odd assortment of parts in the 'Harry Worth', 'Adam Adamant' and 'Troubleshooter' series.

After a while his singing career began to perk up and he played a succession of top cabaret clubs.

Then one day last autumn Barry walked purposefully into the offices of Nems Enterprises with a demonstration disc tucked under his arm. *(Was this recorded at Shield?)* He walked out again a much happier man and is now under a management and agency contract to Nems.

A new record label was also being formed about that time called MCA which was looking for new talent. They offered Barry a contract with the result that his first disc is one of their first releases.

Although he has had several small parts on television, the nearest Barry got to appearing in the role of a singer on television was during the four months he acted as stand-in for Tom Jones and Engelbert Humperdink during rehearsals for 'Top of the Pops'. *Linda Hutchins.*

Evening Telegraph Monday March 11 1968.

They came in their hundreds...

It was a staggering result, "they came in their hundreds," said Mr. G. Drage, manager of Burton Latimer Co-operative Society Ltd's electrical department. He was talking about Saturday's visit to the department of local boy made good, Barry Noble whose first single record was released on Friday.

Barry, whose parents keep the Red Lion at Isham, appeared at the store to sign autographs and sign his new record, "I Can't Forget" released on the MCA Label through NEMS Enterprises the company that launched the Beatles.

Our picture shows Barry with some of his fans.

Barry Noble said, 'I recorded a song called 'I Can't Forget' (written by Don Black). It got played on Radio Luxembourg but didn't sell many copies. I left them and signed with EMI Columbia and recorded a song called 'I Got My Eyes on You' which sold quite well.'

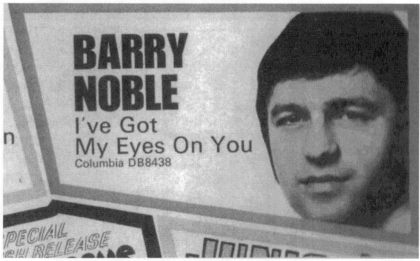

'I've Got My Eyes On You' was recorded in Abbey Rd Studio Two using twenty-five session musicians. Ken Woodman arranged the music and John Burgess produced it.

Barry worked with Steve Fearn's Brass Foundry when he was given his own 30-minute BBC2 show 'Colour Me Pop', broadcast on August 23rd, 1968 and 'In All Directions' made by ITV Birmingham. They also did some Radio 1 sessions together.

Barry's cover of this Tom Paxton song was released in 1969.

Barry was kept busy all through 1969 without quite making the breakthrough into the big time. Further TV appearances and appearances on the continent kept his profile raised.

Fanzine autograph & newspaper cuttings.

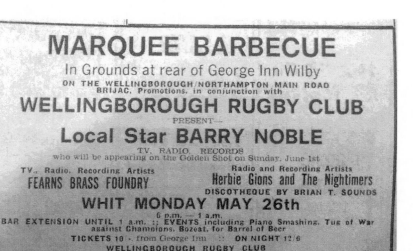

Whit Monday May 26th, 1969.

From the ET August 1969.

Derek kept in close contact with Barry and often accompanied him to the studio. Derek pestered Barry's A&R man to record the Billy Eckstine and Sarah Vaughan classic 'Passing Strangers'.

He knew that the song suited Barry down to the ground and would be a sure-fire hit, but by the time they'd finished prevaricating and recorded it, Mercury records had dusted off the 1957 record master and re-released it. The Vaughan/Eckstine version made the top twenty and Barry's recording was consigned to the B side of his next single.

Steve Fearn and his band accompanied Barry on several trips to the continent. They also collaborated on several songs including the B side of the 'Take Your Time' single that was released in 1970.

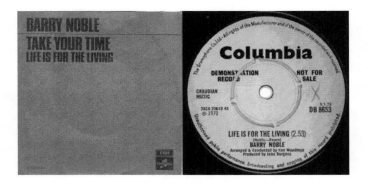

He posted this on a Dr Who fan site. 'I came to London to be a hit recording artist and fell into the acting work as a sideline. I signed a record contract with EMI in 1968 and recorded all my stuff for the next two years at Abbey Road, the same studios as The Beatles. I didn't really have a hit in this country, but I had a few hits abroad and did a lot of shows on the continent. I was travelling around the world quite a lot and the singing career took up the next 15 years.'

CHAPTER 14: RECORDING AT SHIELD
(Part 2)

The authors spent an entertaining couple of hours with Dave Wagg at his Barton Seagrave home. Back in the early 1960s he was the drummer with The Fireflies. They were formed in Wellingborough/Rushden in 1962. The band members included 20-year-old Dave Wagg on drums, 15-year-old Mick Cox on lead guitar, and Dave's younger brother Derek who was 16.

Their first gig was in late 1962 at Doddington Memorial Hall. A rival band was booked to play at the Gloucester Hall in Wellingborough but there was a fire and the show was cancelled. Undaunted, their audience made their way out to Great Doddington and packed the hall (and drank the next-door pub dry.) Dave said that the entrance fee was 2/6d (12 and a half pence) and the band were paid £15 (a lot of money when the average wage was less than £10 a week).

When they first began gigging their kit included a Watkins Dominator amp, a Watkins Copycat tape echo unit, a home-made bass amp and a drum kit that Dave bought in Northampton.

An early 1960s Watkins Dominator and Copicat echo unit.

Dave said that the original lineup was singer, lead guitar, rhythm guitar, bass and drums. When they started out, they played the usual hits of the day. There was very little to distinguish them from all the other bands.

They were based in Wellingborough and Rushden and most of their bookings were either local or south towards Bedford with only the occasional gig in Kettering. They rarely if ever ventured as far north as Corby because of its reputation as a Wild West town.

(DC- When I moved to Northampton in 1974 and formed Left Hand Drive we rarely played in Corby for the same reason.)

After they'd been together for a couple of years, they gave a lift to a long-haired hitchhiker as they travelled to a booking.

His name was John Tyrell and he lived in Barton Seagrave. He had seen the band play a few times and liked what they did.

It turned out that he could play harmonica and later that night joined them on stage to play on a couple of songs. He joined the band and within a few weeks he had bought and taught himself how to play the saxophone.

In the meantime, the band's repertoire had changed to include Motown, Stax and James Brown songs. It set them apart from the other local bands. They became very popular, with bookings both locally and further afield.

In early 1967 they played a Sunday night show at the Granada in Kettering. The Q Men were also on the bill. Derek listened to their set and suggested they come in to Shield and record some tracks.

On April 22nd, 1967 they had a booking supporting Mary Wells and her band at The Gaiety in Ramsey, Cambridge. *(There will be more about the visiting US acts in a later chapter, but it's highly likely that she was a fake.)* After dropping everyone off at their homes Dave didn't get to bed until after 2.00.

The next morning, they made their way to Cambridge Street, arriving at about 11. Dave remembers that there were egg boxes stuck to the walls and ceiling of a room about twenty feet by ten. Everyone set up in the same room (no drum booth).

Dave had a microphone in his bass drum and another overhead. Each of the three vocalists had a mike.

Derek placed mikes in front of the guitar, bass and organ amplifiers, and set up a mike for the sax player. There were nine or ten mikes in all.

Over the next couple of hours, they recorded nine tracks, completely live with no overdubs. They heard nothing more until they were given three acetate LP copies of the session a few weeks later.

The Fireflies finally broke up in October 1967.

Remarkably one of those acetates survived until the late 1990s. When it passed to Dave it was in very poor condition, scratched and dirty.

Derek had long since retired and was living in Broughton. Dave took the disc to him and asked, more in hope than expectation, if Derek could do anything with it.

Derek had been keeping up to date with all the latest digital and computer technology and had invented a gizmo that could remove scratches from the audio. He took Dave's acetate and a few days later gave him back a CD containing the fully restored tracks.

Dave played us a couple of tracks. The band was really tight and tuneful as they played the Vanilla Fudge arrangements of 'You Keep Me Hanging On' and 'Take Me For A Little While.'

They were a great sounding band.

1965   The Fireflies.   1967

CHAPTER 15: THE TIN HAT OPENS

The Tin Hat was a corrugated iron clad steel framed building that had originally been opened in 1900 as the Athletic Club. It was nestled in the shadow of the town's football ground. The facilities were almost non-existent and eventually the decision was taken to open a new club along the road.

WHEN members of Kettering Athletic Club meet in their spacious new premises this weekend you can be sure that the conversation of some of the older members will turn to the old days—to the time when the club began 67 years ago.

Their first home was a corrugated iron building within the football field—a site that remained their home until this weekend. That clubroom's main feature was a large oval bar in the centre of the room. In the middle of it stood a coke stove, the only form of heating.

The club had its struggles. It came near to financial disaster (as the occasion when it had to sell off the ground in which it stood to the Poppies).

But the officers were faced with the fact that the old premises could never be really satisfactory. They were faced, too, with the fact that some of their land would be needed for road improvements. So a bold decision was made. A site was bought for £7,000 and plans begun for a new club.

For years to come officials will tell the story of the trials of the succeeding days when they tried to overcome the obstacles in the way of their venture. One of these was parking. The planning authorities insisted on adequate car parking off the street. So the club plans were re-drawn to allow room for a car park to accommodate 70.

The new building had a large car park and the rear doors opened onto the stage which made loading in very easy for the groups that performed there. It opened for business in April 1967 and the old hut was consigned to history.

A few weeks later Derek's brother Brian reopened The Tin Hat as a music venue. He removed the old central bar and built a stage at one end. It proved to be very popular from the outset, so much so that both Derek and Mavis came in most Saturday nights to help behind the bar. Their daughter Lynda was 4. Mavis' parents were roped in to babysit. Mavis said that it was a hard and hectic lifestyle.

The opening night was June 10th, 1967. It was almost certainly Derek's last gig with the Q-Men. The club opened on Fridays, Saturdays and Sundays with a live band (or two) on a Saturday night and discos on the other nights. This fitted in well with The Works, the other regular music venue in Wellington Street. Their live music nights were on Sunday and Monday nights.

'The Nite People open new discotheque.'
Teenscene by Linda Hutchins

What better way to launch a new discotheque than to book a new and promising group for the first session. Hence The Nite People's appearance when the Tin Hat in Rockingham Road, Kettering, opened on Sunday night. When the Nite People formed in 1965 they hadn't got a clue what to call themselves. After close analysis- they stayed up half the night and slept half the morning- they decided to call themselves- The Nite People. It was a memorable day- it was April 1. In the first year they did most of the spade work for their career. They toured Germany and Austria for four months gleaning valuable experience before returning to their homeland. In October they signed to Avenue Artistes and appointed Terry Rolph as personal manager, and followed this in November by making their first BBC Television appearance. Incidentally, in case you missed the boys on Sunday, there are five of them- Johnny Warwick, vocalist and lead guitar, Frances Gordon, bass; Christopher Ferguson, drummer; Harry Curtis, piano and organ and Patrick Bell, tenor and flute. The boys have had the distinction of touring with the Beach Boys and with Martha and the Vandellas, both of which boosted their national popularity. As yet they have not broken into the charts- but it's not for want of trying. Twelve months ago they made an independent recording with Bob James- an original number by Kirby Small- Martha (of Vandella fame)'s guitarist. Entitled 'Sweet Tasting Wine' it sold well for a first disc. On March 17th this year they released a big soulful single 'Try to Find Another Man'- a number one hit for the Righteous Brothers in America, but that has not happened- yet! The last I heard the factory had to press a new lot of the disc to meet the demand. The Nite People are not kids- Francis is 20 and Chris is 22. The others are all 24, so they are under no illusion about overnight fame, but I feel that given time and the facilities to develop the kind of soul sound that could be among the evergreen names.

Article in the Advertiser June 1967.

Very few photos of the venue exist. The smell of the interior must have been a heady mixture of tobacco smoke and warm beer, and no doubt the floor would have been pretty sticky by the end of the evening.

Roger Kinsey turned up a couple of the posters that were designed by Brian Hindmarch and they are reproduced later in the chapter.

Opening weekend June 1967. No jokes about Yvonne the Limbo Dancer bending over backwards to please her audience perleez!

The disco nights featured Brian (Tompkins Sound) and Mavis' brother Alan (Allan D). They used Derek's Shield disco gear and it wasn't long before they were performing at other well-known venues like the Nag's Head at Wollaston or the George at Wilby.

Mavis wrote:

'Brian used to book some of the most famous soul and Motown bands of the time. Most of the Tompkins family got involved, from Brian's wife (another Mavis), on the door, to his older kids on the cloakroom and glass collecting duties.

121

Derek and I would help behind the bar with serving drinks and glass washing, which involved dunking empty beer glasses into an ice-cold sink full of murky water as fast as we were able.

Our tasks included sweeping the filthy debris and beer-soaked floors and toilets afterwards. Mavis, Brian's wife, had to be a pretty tough cookie, dealing with clashes from mods and rockers etc., and was famous for knocking out one belligerent customer who ended up in hospital!'

Brian's wife Mavis on the door. (John Dark's photo)

Derek later wrote:

'It was always full to capacity every Saturday night, supposedly with around 200-300 punters, but it was more like 600! Brian booked a host of big stars: including Fleetwood Mac and John Mayall's Bluesbreakers.'

In his book 'It's Steel Rock'n Roll to Me' Clive Smith recounts the almost weekly clashes between Kettering and Corby lads outside the venue.

Several people who posted on the Facebook pages also commented on the club's bouncers. It seems that you tangled with them at your peril!

(Appendix One contains a full list of bands that played the Tin Hat between 1967 and the end of 1969.)

Fake bands.

In the mid sixties the Roy Tempest Organisation was one of the UK's biggest music promoters and agents. The Canadians signed with them in late 1966 and went to work backing visiting US acts like Chuck Berry.

However, there was another side to the agency. They regularly brought in unknown US acts and passed them off as Motown groups. The groups were tribute acts, sometimes but not always containing an original band member.

Tempest got around the law by subtly changing their names, calling them 'The Fabulous Temptations' or the 'Original Drifters'.

Bill Pinkney was an original member of The Drifters dating back to 1953 and sang bass on many of their hit records. He and the group toured the UK three times in 1966. The members included Pinkney, first tenor Gerhart Thrasher and baritone Bobby Hendricks. Pinkney was back in the UK in 1967, this time accompanied by three singers who had never been Drifters at all. They were the unknown US band The Invitations. This was the lineup that played the Tin Hat on Friday September 29th.

The music press was soon up in arms. A reporter from Disc took it up with Tempest who argued that the promoters knew only too well they are not getting the real group. He claimed it was OK because he knew of five sets of Drifters touring the US at that time.

Tempest supplied several more acts for the Tin Hat in 1967/8, including 'The Fabulous Temptations' on September 15th, 1967 (actually the Fantastics who had recently changed their name from The Velours).

'James & Bobby Purify' appeared on February 3rd, 1968. It's quite possible that the February 17th appearance by 'Edwin Starr' was yet another tribute act. Tempest also had a 'Mary Wells' and a 'Fontella Bass' act. They were the same singer.

Roger Kinsey remembers going to The Gaiety in Ramsey to see 'The Isley Brothers' in February 1968. Were they the genuine article? Nobody knew what the genuine band looked like, and that was good enough for Tempest.

Motown eventually took legal action against him when they discovered that the Fantastics were being passed off as The Temptations and the resulting court case ended with Tempest's bankruptcy.

Brian Hindmarch's Tin Hat posters 1968

A few Tin Hat 1967 dates

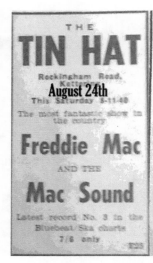

Some more 1968 dates.

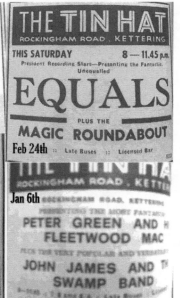

More shows from 1968.

CHAPTER 16: RECORDING AT SHIELD
(Part 3)

The Evening Telegraph ran a full-page article about Derek and Shield Studio in its edition of August 3rd, 1968. Staff Photographer Doug Millhouse took the photographs. The article was written by Linda Hutchins.

In a small shed at the bottom of his garden works Derek Tompkins

BACK-STREET GENIUS OF DISCS

'Derek Tompkins is a genius- he won't tell you that, but hundreds of young people will. And they are the people he has helped on the road to success with his mini-recording studios in Cambridge Street, Kettering.

For unlike the recording crews in the big London studios Derek has the know-how and patience to help the strugglers who have the talent but need the break to get them to the top.

The studios are small and compact and housed in a purpose-built shed at the bottom of the garden.

You have to knock hard on the door, and if recording is in progress you get nothing more than a blast of melody in reply.

The artist's part of the studio is lined with sound-proof boarding so that the tapes are completely isolated from outside distractions.

You'll fall over the odd mike and have to negotiate with care the cleverly woven web of wires on the floor.

There is a smaller room which leads off from the artist's room and it's halfway glazed so that Derek can communicate visually as well as verbally with the recorder.

In this little room is a wealth of panels and contraptions that would have fitted into any Doctor Who episode- and each knob means something different. There's a stopwatch- and the inevitable packet of cigarettes.

Let the recording session begin. The subjects- Steve Fearn, Freddie Jordan, Barry Sutton and Mick Poulton- are session men from Leicester. Their job- to record the brass section of a demo tape for a composition by Northampton song-writer Jo Ryan.

They crowd into Derek's control room to listen to the melody and pick up instructions from Jo. Their minds retain the tune. They pick up their instruments and play- direct.

But that's not the end of things by a long chalk. Jo wants that 'funky' sound from the brass, and it has to be balanced accordingly. The pitch and volume of each instrument, banjo, clarinet, trombone and trumpet can be varied and balanced.

The staccato of the banjo must be picked out and emphasised and their timing must be perfect.

The boys may play one piece a dozen times- and each time it will be balanced, recorded and played back until Jo is satisfied.

The rest of the backing and the vocal are recorded at other times on separate tapes. This is where Derek's genius comes in. It is up to him to edit and collate the best parts of each recording to fit them perfectly together so that Jo will have a good tape to take to the publishers.

The boys have had a break and London song-writer Frank Kinsella appears on the scene- he's heard the quality of Derek's tapes and he's come to see the master at work.

Leicester sessionmen Freddie Jordan, Barry Sutton, Mick Poulton and Steve Fearn in session at the studios.

'Honestly some of his work is fabulous compared with even the top recording boys in London,' enthused Frank in a thick Irish brogue. 'I've heard master tapes of Derek's and I'd like him to record for me.'

Frank has penned all the Spectrum hits and was responsible for their latest gimmicky recording of 'London Bridge is Coming Down'.

Steve Fearn is a craftsman in his own right as leader of Fearn's Brass Foundry from Leicester- tipped as one of the Midland's most professional dance hall groups.

Steve does his own writing and works closely with Derek on production. At the recording session he picked up a borrowed banjo for the first time and began strumming away as if it was second nature to him- 'I quite fancy myself as Leicester's answer to the Black & White Minstrels' he quipped.

Local pop singer Barry Noble, whose latest waxing of the Barry Mason-Les Reed number 'I've Got My Eyes On You' is at last making headway in the charts has a lot to be grateful for at Shield Studio.

In fact, almost every pop group in the town owes something to modest Derek, who has loaned them part of his genius to make them a success. He's their friend who is interested in their future, he's there to help them and not just sit behind the controls like a disinterested nameless dummy.'

6   Evening Telegraph.   Monday, August 5, 1968.

Freddie, Barry and Mick.

130

Derek at the controls at Shield Studio in August 1968.

Derek's reputation as a top recording engineer and producer and manufacturer of quality amplifiers and speakers was growing. So how come he was working all the hours under the sun and yet he still wasn't making any money?

CHAPTER 17: STEVE FEARN

We met up with Steve Fearn in a Market Harborough hostelry one autumn afternoon where we spent an entertaining couple of hours reminiscing about the far-off fifties, sixties and seventies and Steve's part in this story.

Steve's first band drawing a crowd. Market Harborough 1959.

Steve Fearn's introduction to music was in 1955 when he first heard Bill Haley and the Comets' recording of 'Rock around the Clock'.

Mavis' friend Yvonne said that Steve told her that it was her uncle Bob who introduced him to the guitar and taught him. Steve said that he might never have picked up the guitar were it not for him.

Steve played his first gig at the Liberty Hall (now the Harborough Theatre) on the same day that he got his first guitar. He got the guitar in the afternoon then rushed home to learn some chords before that evening's show.

His first band was a skiffle group called The Diamonds (later changed to the Double Diamonds because there was another local band with the same name.)

Steve's first ever recording was at the Abbey Road Studios in London. He was only 14. The Double Diamonds had played a barbeque party in nearby Arthingworth. The chief executive of Columbia Records was there. When Steve played him an instrumental, the first thing he'd ever written on guitar, the CEO was so impressed he invited the band to go down to Abbey Road to record the following Monday.

Russ Conway was recording when they arrived at the studio. Once he had finished the band set up and prepared to record. Their bass player had only recently switched from T-chest bass to double bass. After the band had finished recording the engineer took Steve off to one side and told him 'You seem to be one of the few in the band who actually knows what's going on. You realise that your bass player is playing nothing- just noise.' What notes he did make bore no resemblance to the tune. Steve remembers that he was a lovely fellow and a great organiser, but was this a timely reminder that enthusiasm is no substitute for ability?

Steve stayed in Market Harborough until he was 18. Once he'd passed his driving test he moved to Leicester and joined an Irish Showband. Steve said that they were fabulous musicians and as he got to know them, they really nurtured him. He stayed with them for about two years.

He started his own group in 1963 or 64, a trio called The Executives that eventually expanded to be a nine-piece band in the style of bands like the Alan Price Set, Hal C Blaine or Herbie Goins and the Nightimers, all very popular late 60s groups. Steve always surrounded himself with good musicians so the band would have been very tight.

In 1964 Steve took The Executives to Kettering to record a demo with Derek in the workshop at the back of the Regent Street shop. He said that the studio was very primitive and so small that the band had to stand elbow to elbow to record. The keyboard player was Bill Coleman. More about him later.

Steve never recorded at The Windmill but went to the new Shield studio in 1966 to record the demo for 'Don't Change It'.

They got a recording contact with Decca on the back of it, and the song was rerecorded with an arrangement by Ivor Raymonde and released in 1968.

While it wasn't a hit, it became a Northern Soul favourite and can still be heard on the BBC's 'Homes under the Hammer' TV show from time to time.

Steve said that he preferred the version of 'Don't Change It' that was recorded at Derek's. While the Decca version was more polished and used a 20-piece band, all top musicians, the Shield recording seemed more real with a raw edge.

He spent a lot of time at Shield and Beck over the next few years and introduced many players who went on to greater things in the 70s. The Brass Foundry backed Barry Noble when he appeared on BBC2's 'Colour Me Pop' in August 1968. Regrettably only the audio survives. It can be found on YouTube.

He also co-composed a few songs with Barry that were recorded in London and released in the early 70s. He was also responsible for the legendary Sunday night sessions at the Bath Hotel in Shearsby in Leicestershire.

Ex-Spencer Davis Group drummer Pete York made the trip over from Birmingham every Sunday to join in the fun. He became yet another regular at Shield and Beck.

Steve said that Derek was really helpful and taught him such a lot and even today still says he never charged enough for his advice, expertise and services.

In 1968 his band went to Shield and recorded nine tracks for a proposed album that was never released. Very few acetates survive but one turned up on Discogs recently. The seller wanted £800 for it. Steve said he would have to go through his cupboards to see if there were anymore lurking there!

The tracks included covers of Johnny Mathis, Jackie Wilson and Curtis Mayfield songs; some instrumentals including Soul Limbo by Booker T and the MGs and three originals by Steve.

In the mid 1970s Brass Foundry released a limited-edition LP that they sold at their gigs. All 1000 sold out quickly. The cover photograph was taken at Loughborough Station on the soon to be reopened Great Central Railway.

The changing musical landscape and the rise of punk put an end to the band. Steve teamed up with ex-Jigsaw drummer and vocalist Des Dyer to form a cabaret duo called Fingersnfumbs, which continues to entertain audiences at the time of writing.

"Now I Taste the Tears" —a Buzz Clifford song — is performed on Decca by the described as a power-packed **Fearns Brass Foundry.** It's semi-ballad—in other words it's somewhat original.

COMEDY

The group comes from Leicester and in their comedy flavoured stage act they are dressed in uniforms which at one time belonged to Market Harborough Town Band. "Love Sink and Drown" is the title on the other side.

CHAPTER 18: BUSY BUSY BUSY!

Mavis drew this cartoon of Derek in his workshop.

In January 1968 Derek enrolled on a 13-week course at the London Polytechnic. Every Thursday he travelled down to London by train to learn more about recording studio techniques. Mavis drove him to and from the station. He arrived home tired out from the travelling, had his dinner and started work in the repair shop or down at the studio until early in the morning. Mavis remembers that he worked very long hours.

Derek's recording prowess had soared in the small workshop at the bottom of the garden in Cambridge Street that used to be part of Mavis' father's Cytringan Welder Company's factory. They were still living above the shop in Regent Street, and recordings would often last all day and into the night.

Sometimes Mavis would cook dinner and take it to the studio for Derek, or else cook late at night when he finally got home. She said that he'd often come home in the wee small hours, eat his dinner in bed and fall asleep, sometimes with his mouth still full. He was building Shield amplifiers and speaker cabinets in the factory, repairing TVs and record players at the shop as well as running the recording studio until all hours and helping out at the Tin Hat Club most weekends.

Mavis kept a diary in 1968 and it gives a clue to how busy he was.

January 11th — 1st day at London Poly.
January 18th — London Poly recording course.
January 20th — All day recording session.
January 20th — (night) Helping at Tin Hat (The Triads).
January 25th — London Poly.
Jan 27th — Tin Hat.
Jan 28th- — Studio all day, Tin Hat evening.
Jan 29th- — Steve Fearn recording.
Jan 31st — Q Men reunion dinner. Derek was given a silver cigarette case as a thank you gift from the band.
Feb 2nd- — Studio.
Feb 3rd- — Tin Hat. James & Bobby Purify.
Feb 4th- — Studio all day then Tin Hat.
Feb 8th — London Poly.
Feb 11th — Studio.
Feb 15th — London Poly.
Feb 17th — George Hotel dance with Q Men.
Feb 17th — Edwin Starr at The Tin Hat.
Feb 20th — Studio.
Feb 22nd — London Poly.
Feb 24th — The Equals at Tin Hat.
Mar 8th — Steve Fearn recording session.

During 1968 and 69 a great many groups recorded at Shield. Several went on to greater things. Here are a few of their stories.

Spell originated from Bedford and gigged the local clubs and pubs back in 67/68. A session was organised to record a few of guitarist Dave King's songs at Shield Studios in Kettering. Dave was friends with Derek, so a session was arranged in studio downtime. Only one acetate disc of the session survived, containing three original songs and a cover of Love's 'She Comes In Colours.' The three originals were released on an EP by TOR Records of Litchfield in 2015.

The only acetate of Spell's session at Shield and the TOR reissue.

In a 2015 interview with Lenny Helsing for the psychedelicbaby.com website Dave King said:

'The studio date was very natural for me, as I was a great friend of Derek Tompkins, a lovely person with a great studio. He taught me lots of things, including how to build compressors! I got studio time to write, so Spell got a session! Derek's studio was good, relaxed, thanks to him. He had a stutter, which manifested itself on the talk back. Some patience was required.'

Legay were another top Leicester band who recorded at Shield. Two of the tracks were recently released on a 4 track EP by Circle Records.

Legay, sleeve notes and replica acetate disc (in vinyl).

Back in 2013 Brian Hemming wrote about Legay on his Wordpress site. He knew the band well, having been to junior school with their guitarist/vocalist and main songwriter Robin Pizer. In his opinion they could have been one of the biggest bands in Britain. They had looks, style and music and all they lacked was that final, tiny bit of musical polish, and a really good producer.

Their 1968 single on Fontana failed to make the charts and sometime after their December 3rd session at Shield they changed their name to Gypsy, who went on to release a couple of LPs on the United Artists label in 1971 and 72.

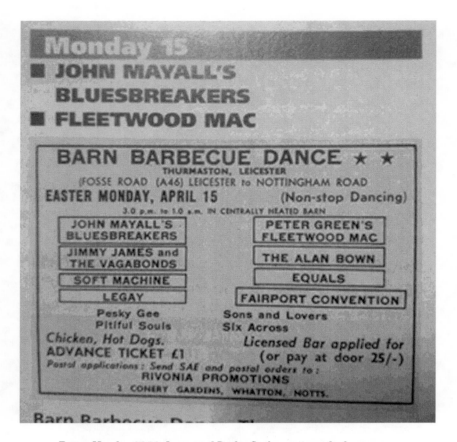

Easter Monday 1968. Legay and Pesky Gee! were in exalted company.

In November 1968 the Q Men recorded a song called 'Peanut Vendor' and sent the demo to The Beatles Apple Corp Company. Their reply was swift and to the point.

From Apple

Ref: IOI8.

Mr. Derek Tompkins,
I3 Regent St,
Kettering,   I4th November I968.

Dear Mr. Tompkins,

We are very touched that you should have
chosen us to consider your creative work
and we want to assure you that we have
treated it with an interest which matches
the effort you have put in.

We regret, however, that we are not at this
time able to proceed with what you have in
mind and we know that you will accept from
us that our rejection in no way implies any
inadequacy in your work, for the submission
of which we offer you our renewed thanks.

Very best wishes and kindest regards,
we continue to be

                              Yours sincerely,

                              For Apple Publishing Ltd.

Unlike many of his contemporaries, Derek built, and hand wired much of the equipment including the mixing desk. The recordings he made were every bit the equal in quality and in many cases superior. Derek's desire to produce the best possible recordings for his clients remained undiminished.

It gave them a glimpse of the standard required to make a record that was suitable to be released and it also gave them the experience that would be invaluable should they make it to the big London studios.

1963   1968

According to Wiki, US record producer and songwriter Kim Fowley came to the UK in the mid 60s and persuaded Leicester based group The Farinas to change their name to Family. We know that both groups recorded with Derek but haven't been able to discover whether Fowley was present at any of the sessions. He went on to discover and manage The Runaways, the all-girl group that featured Joan Jett on guitar.

As Derek's reputation grew many songwriters including Kettering based Robin Goodfellow beat a path to his door to record their songs in his studio in a quiet back street.

CHAPTER 19:
ROBIN GOODFELLOW & NICK EVANS

Robin Goodfellow is a songwriter who was active for about ten years in the 60s and 70s. He started writing songs when he was in his late teens. He knew Mick Smith from Rothwell who had a famous brother called Jim Dale. During 1965/6 Jim was starring in the 'Carry On' films and hosting ITV's 'Thank Your Lucky Stars' weekly TV pop music programme. Robin had three songs he wanted to play to him so got Jim's address from Mick and headed down to Pinner in West London.

Robin said- 'Mick told me that he lived in Pinner. So, I went down there, got off the train, walked out of the station and asked the first person I saw if he knew where Jim Dale lived. He said, 'just down there- number 58.' I knocked on the door and Jim answered it. I told him that I knew his brother Mick. He said that you were looking for new material. (I made that bit up) I had a reel to reel tape recorder at that time and played the songs to him.

Jim said that he quite liked the last one but not the lyrics. Shall we rewrite them? So, he wrote some more lyrics and said that he would send the song to his publisher. I never heard any more from that- but I can say that my first song was written for Jim Dale. He did give me a bit of advice though. He said that whatever you do make your demo as good as possible. The recording executives have absolutely no imagination whatsoever.'

Nick Evans has known Robin since childhood. His parent's garden backed on to Robin's and they often chatted over the garden wall. Nick started out as a guitarist. He played lead guitar on Ann & Ray Brett's first recording session at The Windmill Club early in 1965. (See page 56.)

Nick's guitar set up.

Nick started out playing lead guitar on a Rosetti Airstream guitar through a Vox AC15 amplifier. He then changed to bass guitar, playing a Hofner Beatles bass through a Vox T60 amplifier. He later switched to a Gibson EBO bass.

His regular drummer was John Gilbert and they played together in many bands through the rest of the decade including The Impressions, Freddie 'Fingers' Lee and The Upper Hand, The Stumblin' and Fallin' Blues Band, and T-Byrd's Chicago Blues Band. Stu Edson aka 'Tich' was their vocalist in many of the bands.

Nick remembers spending a Sunday recording with Robin at the Windmill Club. He disliked the experience so much that he listed it as his hate item on his EMI biography! They also recorded at Derek's shop in Regent Street, not in the workshop out the back but in full view of passers-by in the shop! Nick said they also recorded at Advision before settling on Regent Sound in Denmark Street at about the same time as he recorded 'Bossy Boss' with Freddie 'Fingers' Lee and The Upper Hand at Regent Sound in 1966.

During the late 1960s Robin recorded as Robin Tracy. Although he was a keyboard player he rarely if ever played on the sessions. He usually recorded his songs with drummer John Gilbert; Nick on bass and occasional guitar; lead guitarist Tony Bird and singer Stu Edson (aka Tich). Roy Smith, singer with Peter, Paul & Egbert also sang on some of the demos as did ex Fireflies vocalist Derek Wagg.

Robin hired a minibus to take the musicians and equipment down to London. The recording sessions were in four-hour blocks. The larger studios held three sessions a day and you had to get set up, record your song and clear the studio within your allotted time.

It was a high-pressure environment and not for the faint hearted. Linda Hutchins mentioned this in her 1966 article about 'Recording the Fireflies' that is reprinted in Chapter 7. She recognised that the time spent recording a demo with Derek would pay dividends later.

Robin also hired a village hall where he taught the song to the musicians. Once they had mastered it, he booked studio time at Regent Sound. Hiring a rehearsal room, van and recording studio wasn't cheap and he still had to pay to have the tape copied to an acetate disc. All too often he sent the disc off to a record company but never heard back from them.

Freddie 'Fingers' Lee's 'Bossy Boss' was released on the Columbia label in September 1966. It was recorded at Regent Sound. Freddie's musicians on the session were Nick on bass, John Gilbert on drums and Tam MacDonald on guitar. Tam used an amplifier that Derek had made for him. It had a built-in fuzz unit. (Have you heard the Rolling Stones recording of 'Satisfaction'? That's what fuzz sounds like.) Nick remembers that Ian Patterson (aka Ian Hunter) sang backing vocals and songwriter Tony Macaulay was in charge of the session. Nick said that Tony was very friendly and likeable and bursting with song ideas.

TAM STONE (real name Thomas MacDonald) is 21 years old and was born in Motherwell, Scotland on July 26, 1945. After leaving school at 15 had jobs as a shop worker, steelworker, shoe operative and navvy. Is also musically self-taught and plays lead and bass guitar, bagpipes and a little piano. Turned professional in February 1965 and joined the group in May of this year. Likes football and living. Dislikes untidy people and being broke. Wants to be successful in show business. With light brown hair and blue eyes, Tam is 5ft. 10½ins. tall.

NICK EVANS (real name Graham Nicholas Evans) is 19 years old and was born in Kettering, Northants, on January 20, 1947. Had various jobs on leaving school at 15. Nick plays bass and lead guitar and was with various groups including one called The Impressions for two years. Six months ago Freddie asked him to join The Upper Hand. Likes Chinese food, beer, The Hollies, watching TV with his wife and playing records. Hates recording on Sundays. Would like to make his mark as a musician. With chestnut-brown hair and blue/green eyes he is 5ft. 8ins tall.

JOHN GILBERT is 23 years old and was also born in Kettering on January 6, 1943. Had many jobs on leaving school at 15. Taught himself to play drums and worked with several bands before joining The Upper Hand in April. Likes listening to top jazz drummers and The Hollies. Dislikes being broke. Wants to be a success. Has light brown hair, green eyes and is 6ft. 1ins. tall.

"BOSSY BOSS" by FINGERS LEE AND THE UPPER HAND is coupled with "DON'T RUN AWAY" and released on Columbia DB8002.

From the EMI Press Release September 1966.

Nick also recorded on a session with Jimmy Pollock (aka Gidian) at Hollick & Taylor in Birmingham that featured John Gilbert on drums, Nick on bass and the whole brass section of the Birmingham Philharmonic Orchestra (moonlighting?)

Nick Evans' set up. Hofner Beatle bass and Vox T60 amplifier.

Gibson EBO bass guitar.

Elizabeth Plaistere remembers when Gidian was recording his first record 'There Isn't Anything' at Hollick & Taylor. Ken Dodd must have been there and when he heard the record been played, he asked who was singing.

Ked Dodd was very impressed and met up with Gidian for publicity photos, telling him that he would be his protégé. He described Gidian's voice as being 'plum-shush'. Ken's agent wanted to sign him up as a cabaret artiste, but Gidian turned the offer down.

In 1966 Robin heard from Barry Noble that Derek was opening a new studio. Robin decided that it was a lot less bother than travelling down to Regent Sound so began recording at Shield in Cambridge Street.

Nick remembers that in 1967 many of Robin's songs were influenced by psychedelic music. He wrote songs with unusual titles like 'Left-Handed Sort of Dream'. According to Nick the first verse began 'I walked down a path that was made of margarine'.

Robin recorded the tracks at Shield but then took the master tapes down to the London Weekend TV studio in London to be mixed and mastered. He always took Jim Dale's advice and made his demos as good as possible.

Robin eventually got fed up with sending acetates down to the record companies and never hearing back, so he began to deliver them in person. He once cold called Mickie Most at his home to hand over his latest demo. It made no difference!

One day Robin was having a track mixed in the recently refurbished Studio Two in Abbey Road.

George Martin walked in and asked him what he thought of the changes. This was the first time that Robin had been in the studio, so he just blurted out that they were 'a big improvement'.

Derek Wagg sang on this Robin Tracy (Goodfellow) demo.

Nick stopped recording for Robin in the late 60s and took a couple of years off before resuming his musical career.

Robin used a different group of musicians when he recorded at Derek's Beck Studio and his persistence finally paid off when he had three singles released in the early 70s:

'Hey Did You Know You've Got Your Face On Upside Down?' was co-written with Steve Fearn and released by Gidians League on the Parlophone label in 1972. Guitarist Tam MacDonald and drummer Robert Gowan played on this track.

Robin had two singles released under his own name. 'Why Am I Waiting' (on the Pye label) was released in 1973; and 'You Know Me Now/I'm Suddenly Alive' (Dawn) in 1974.

CHAPTER 20: DIABOLUS AND SKINNY CAT

Richard Rhodes has fond memories of working with Derek. When he was living in Oxford in the mid sixties, he was a regular at the Stage Club. One night (probably in 1967) he saw an early power trio by the unlikely name of Three Ways of Doing It. The venue manager was being awkward about paying them but by the end of the night Richard had got them their fee in full and he and his business partner Patricia Cole had become their managers.

Patricia remembers meeting the band when they were students at Headington Technical College (now part of Oxford Brookes University). She had contacts in the music business through their company Rhodes Hudson and they worked hard to promote the band.

During 1967 and 68 the band played the Oxford college circuit supporting groups as diverse as Cream, The Nice and the Alan Price Set. Richard remembers that they were once supported by Jethro Tull in one of that band's first ever gigs.

One show sticks in Patricia's memory. It was the time they played a students union evening at Headington Tech supporting Arthur Brown. She said, 'the boys were cranking the volume up and Arthur Brown almost set fire to the stage during his set.' Patricia remembers that the group members were notoriously unpredictable, and their riotous behaviour was legendary. Patricia added-

'We started Rhodes Hudson Ltd in 1965-6 after my father died. I was going to study Fine Art/Sculpture but couldn't afford the fees. I had been making skirts and trousers with off cuts from the tannery college to sell to other students so Richard suggested we start the leather clothing company.

We began in 28 Eskdaill Street, Kettering, a very dilapidated terraced house with no heating. I had one industrial sewing machine and a cutting table.

We later moved to a three-storey factory at Gold End, Kettering, near the old Kings Arms pub. Morrisons supermarket was later built on the site.'

On August 2nd, 1967 The Evening Telegraph ran a double page article on them. The author isn't named.

'If enterprise could be weighed and cost £1 an ounce, Richard Rhodes and Patricia Cole would be millionaires by now. Ten months ago, they worked on an idea of making suede and leather clothes in a small building at 28 Eskdaill Street Kettering.

A month later they were backed financially and formed Rhodes Hudson, a limited company, and now they have negotiated with the Board of Trade to export their garments.

Patricia, who lives at 1 Primrose Close Kettering is 19. She attended art school for three years to study to be a teacher. Then she met Richard (22), a leather technician from Buckinghamshire who had been studying at Northampton Technical College. Together they hatched up the business.

It was tricky at first. Patricia made the garments which were sold to friends, but the suede miniskirts which were very popular at the time weren't very profitable. So they decided to branch out and now they will make you anything from a full-length evening gown in leather to a micro-skirted bush suit, made to measure in any shade you wish.

The leather comes from Buckinghamshire and Patricia adapts basic patterns to suit the customer. She has recently completed a cowboy jacket complete with fringe in lilac suede.

'It's not difficult to make the garments' she told the Evening Telegraph. 'I didn't really have any training in dressmaking, but suede and leather are so much easier to make up than ordinary dress fabric.

Much of the garment can be stuck and using proper machines it's easier to sew because it won't slip or stretch.'

Few of the garments are sold locally. Most are too advanced fashion-wise to appeal to local youngsters although anything at all fashionable or otherwise can be made.

Richard handles the business side. He knows exactly where the competition is and how to cope with it. In most business circles he is accepted despite his youth but there are still some people who tend to think that because he is young, he must be irresponsible.

He has the foresight and the fashion contacts to know what will be 'in' in the coming months and plan accordingly.

Incidentally a quick peep into the future promises leather gear in luminous pinks, oranges, lemons and limes- but they may be very expensive because of demand.

Richard and Patricia plan to expand. Within six months they hope to have moved into a bigger open-plan building with possibly a showroom.

They hope to employ more staff, but above all they want to break into the export business.'

In December 1967 Three Ways of Doing It were support to Skip Bifferty at the regular Monday Beat '67 night at Kettering Working Men's Club in Wellington Street.

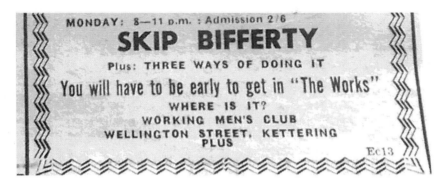

'Three Ways' later expanded to a four piece when they added a keyboard player. In 1969 they got a booking at the Tin Hat and needed a name. They called themselves Pink Cheeks for the gig and then set about finding a new name to go with their new musical direction.

Richard felt that the band needed to cut a demo in order to secure a record and agency deal. He knew about Derek's Shield studio and booked a session in the summer of 1969. The band recorded four or five tracks and had acetates cut.

Richard remembers that Derek had a curious way of announcing the start of a recording.

He simply said 'Here here here it comes' which caused a great deal of mirth and mickey taking by the band on account of his pronounced stutter.

The band members were Tony Hadfield on bass, John Hadfield on guitar and vocals, Ellwood von Seibold on drums and John Laws on keyboards. Patricia said that Ellwood slept on the top floor of the Gold End factory for several months around the time of the recording.

Patricia's friend John Hawken (keyboard player with the Nashville Teens) introduced her to the agent who booked the acts for London clubs like The Revolution, Blazes and Tiles and he booked the group regularly. She was also good friends with Roundhouse DJ Jeff Dexter, and this also helped promote the group.

Richard took the Shield acetate down to London and played it to as many people as he could reach.

Someone arranged for two days' recording time at De Lane Lea studios. That session got them an agency deal with NEMS enterprises and a chance to record their album with Shel Talmy producing. His list of credits included recording The Who and The Kinks.

They secured a publishing deal with Brian Morrison's Lupus Music through Patricia's contacts, joining Syd Barrett, The Pink Floyd and The Pretty Things on their artist roster. John Laws left the band and was replaced by multi-instrumentalist Philip Howard and his flute and saxophone playing added a new dimension to their sound.

Richard was living in a cottage in Furnace Lane, Finedon Sidings. Ellwood had moved from the factory to live next door. The band played a lot of shows supporting Mott the Hoople and their drummer Dale Griffin (aka Buffin) became a close friend and often stayed there. Other guests included Family's Roger Chapman, guitarist Jim Cregan, singer Linda Lewis and acoustic trio America who later had a huge hit with 'Horse with no Name'.

While all this was happening Richard and the band had a meeting with Shel Talmy. He told them that he didn't like the De Lane Lea tapes and wanted to rerecord the album at Sound Techniques in Chelsea.

(This was where Pink Floyd's first two singles and Jethro Tull's first LP (This Was) were recorded. Fairport Convention, Steeleye Span, Nick Drake and Sandy Denny also recorded there.)

Meanwhile Richard took the De Lane Lea tapes around the record companies. He got a good reaction from Charisma's Tony Stratton Smith who told him he was looking at Diabolus seriously along with two other groups- Genesis and Van der Graaf Generator but wanted to hear the Sound Techniques tapes.

Richard later said: 'For some inexplicable reason the re-recorded result was different to the point of not being as good and you know who Tony chose!' Charisma signed Van Der Graaf and Genesis and the rest, they say, is history.

Shel Talmy had paid for the session so owned the tapes, but Ellwood had kept a copy of the first De Lane Lea recording. The Sound Techniques recording was released in Germany in 1971. It's a bone of contention that the band never received a penny for their efforts.

A few years ago, the German album was re-released by a small record label and once again the band members never received payment. How many other bands were ripped off in this way back in the sixties and seventies?

We may never know. Ellwood's copy of the De Lane Lea album is being prepared for possible future release in vinyl format, so it's possible that we haven't heard the last of Diabolus.

Richard Rhodes now lives in Thailand. He recently visited Patricia at her home and posed for this photograph.

A couple of years ago an unnamed acetate was discovered by Barry Noble. He passed it on to Chris McGranaghan of TOR (Those Old Records) and a start was made to identify the group who recorded it. Eventually Richard Rhodes confirmed that it was Diabolos' Shield recording from 1969 and plans are being made to release a limited-edition vinyl LP on the TOR label at some time in the future.

Bernie Marsden and Shield Studio.

In 1968 or 69 Richard promoted some concerts at Buckingham Town Hall. The support group was Skinny Cat featuring a young Bernie Marsden on guitar and vocal.

Richard suggested that they visit Derek's studio to make a demo. They recorded with Derek at Shield and Beck three times in all.

Whitesnake's million selling guitarist and song writer is yet another to add to the list of musicians who began their careers with Derek. Bernie wrote in the April 2018 issue of Guitarist Magazine:

'The first recording studio I ever used was in 1969 in Kettering in Northamptonshire, it was called Shield Studios. My band at the time was Skinny Cat and we had saved some of our gig money to record.

People had been saying how good we were and that we should record something. Foolishly, but with humility, we believed them and committed to a Saturday session in the studio. Well, it was just one afternoon really as the budget only ran to about four hours. During that time, we recorded two songs. I had been in some personal turmoil before the day as I was the lead singer as well as guitarist. What the rest of the band didn't know was that I had never really written any words for the original material we were playing at the time.

This didn't really matter on stage as I made it up as we went along, and I always had a strong chorus line. However, this was of zero use in a recording studio. I decided to record a song by an American band called Rhinoceros instead of one of our own.

The second song was inevitably a slow blues one, an original one by yours truly, the lyrics were all about 'searching for my baby' and 'I left my baby this morning'. You get the drift. Looking back, we were not ready to record at all.

We found that out at about 7pm on the Saturday evening. It was not the greatest recording session, and the outcome is an incredibly rare 45rpm disc. I still have the one and only copy!

The photos from this session were much better than the record. But I had been inside a studio and I loved the experience.

'From Skinny Cat to the great Whitesnake, what a journey!' Bernie Marsden.

I read somewhere that one of the members of Queen (John Deacon) made his first recordings at Shield so I'm in very good company.

We recorded straight to a Revox stereo machine, and the playback sounded wonderful to me. True stereo was a rare experience in those days, and although the engineer had limited resources, what he had sound-wise was very good as far as I was concerned.

We returned to the studio a year later for two more sessions, this time a little more lyrically prepared, but by no means perfect. The second time, all the apprehensions and nerves were gone, and I looked forward to the creativity of the medium. The second and third sessions were good, but stayed unreleased until the 2000s on my anthology album. From Skinny Cat to the great Whitesnake, what a journey!'

And it all began with Derek Tompkins at Shield.

In the late 1960s Charlie Hill played drums in a band with Bernie. He wrote on the Facebook page:

'We only did about six gigs stretched over a year, in between his many trips to London seeking 'the big time'. Bernie called the band 'The James Watt Compassion'.

Now I'm not too sure what that was supposed to represent, possibly his spelling wasn't that great, and he meant 'compression', which would make more sense, given James Watt invented the steam engine.

Anyway, a while later, it must have been '68 or '69, I came to Derek's studio to record with my new band, 'Musrum', and Derek said, 'I had Bernie Marsden in here last week- what a guitarist'. I don't recall the actual date. I lost touch with Bernie but two years ago, he came to see me to deliver a copy of his book, 'Where's My Guitar', in which I have a brief mention. None the less, that's my small claim to fame!'

John Mayall in Kettering.

Patricia Cole remembers making a pair of made to measure leather trousers for blues singer John Mayall. He travelled up by train and she picked him up at the station. He stayed for two or three days, sleeping on the top floor of the factory. One evening he had dinner at Patricia's mum's house but neglected to tell them that he was a vegetarian. Her mum served up liver and onions.

In August 1968 Patricia went to the Decca studio in West Hampstead with Mayall's then drummer Colin Allen. They were recording 'Blues from Laurel Canyon'; the last album Mayall would make for the company. Patricia thought that everyone seemed on edge. Shortly afterwards the group disbanded and Mayall moved to California where he spent the next ten years. Mayall's band played the Tin Hat on September 8th, 1967 and earned a great review in the following week's Advertiser.

Explosion of music- the spell binding Blues Breakers.

'Puny words alone cannot possibly express the brilliance of the performance by John Mayall's Blues Breakers at the Tin Hat on Saturday.

Connoisseurs of blues were able to leave the club newly inspired by their fantastic sound, writes Linda Hutchins.

Smoother than double cream and more liquid than best French brandy, blues filled the air leaving the audience spellbound, and inwardly screaming for more as physical expression exploded into music.

Not being an expert on blues it is difficult to analyse the feelings behind this group and their music, but it does not take an expert to recognise their tenacity and perfection of balance.

Conjuring up patterns of sleepy style Chicago clubs packed with blues singing negroes (sic) there was an uncanny atmosphere as if something which had been bottled up for years had suddenly been let loose to envelope the soul.

There is only one comparison I can draw and that's with negro blues singers Brownie McGhee, Sonny Terry and Big Bill Broonzy the blues masters of the old school to whom blues are just a second nature.

To the Blues Breakers, without that natural instinct, the effort of making that kind of music could have proved a very synthetic disaster- it wasn't- it was a dream.

The most recent addition to the Blues Breakers is (bass) guitarist Paul Williams- poached from Zoot Money's Big Roll Band when it crashed last month, and what an addition. Like a falling guillotine Paul slotted straight into the band, clean and experienced.

Blues may not be everyone's kind of scene, but if you have got room to appreciate it you'll have to search the world to find anyone as soul satisfying as John Mayall's Blues Breakers.'

(Paul Williams was a bass player and he replaced John McVie in the band. The lead guitarist was Mick Taylor.)

CHAPTER 21: PESKY GEE! / BLACK WIDOW

In the late 60s many of Derek's clients hailed from Leicester. Some came over on Steve Fearn's recommendation, and other bands regularly played venues in Kettering and Corby and heard about the studio by word of mouth. The newspaper articles also helped with the publicity. Derek wasn't one for self publicity but it's not beyond the realms of possibility that when he was helping out at the Tin Hat he took the opportunity to speak to the bands.

On March 23rd and July 27th, 1968 Pesky Gee! headlined the Tin Hat. A few weeks later they recorded some demos from their live show at Shield Studio. That session ultimately resulted in a contract with Pye Records.

The original line up was Kay Garrett lead vocals; Kip Trevor vocals/guitar/harmonica; Chris Dredge guitar; Bob Bond bass; Clive Box drums/piano; Alan Hornsby on brass and Clive Jones sax/flute. Kip Trevor had been a one-time member of Corby band The Invaders.

In an interview published on the Marmalade Skies website (www.marmalade-skies.co.uk) sax player Clive Jones explained how they were discovered in Warrington by Malcolm Rabbit who introduced himself as a songwriter with London management. The next afternoon they learned Malcolm's song 'A Place Of Heartbreak' and a few days later they signed up with his management firm and began their recording career. Malcolm's song was the 'B' side of their single, a cover of Vanilla Fudge's 'Where Is My Mind'. After it failed to set the charts alight guitarist Chris Dredge left the band. He was replaced by Jim Gannon.

Clive said that the Pesky Gee! LP was recorded in dead studio time at PYE studios. It took four hours from beginning to end. All those thousands of miles playing all those gigs, coupled with the recent experience gained from recording at Shield meant that the group was able to get each song down in only one take- warts and all. They later found they had been smuggled into the studio and the sessions were never paid for.

Clive said that the group were very fond of the exclamation mark at the end of their name because nobody else had one. Their management rang the record label and told them to make sure they put it on the album at the end of their name.

Pye decided to call the album 'Exclamation Mark' instead.

The band had started out as a Soul/R&B group in Leicester in 1967 during the Summer of Love. Their repertoire evolved over the next couple of years to include songs by the Vanilla Fudge, Julie Driscoll, The Crazy World of Arthur Brown and Steppenwolf. The album's release and poor sales put an end to that phase of their career and after a meeting with their management the decision was taken to change their name and record an album of original material.

At that time there was an interest in the occult and following a suggestion from their drummer Clive Box to make a black magic album, Jim Gannon took on the task of composing the music. In September 1969 the band booked into Shield Studio to record the demo tracks. Several names were thrown into the hat and the band chose Black Widow. Mavis recorded in her diary that this happened on September 25th.

CBS loved the demos and agreed to release an album. As usual the demo recording was rejected because the company thought they could do better. Clive kept his copy of the 1969 demo acetate as a memento.

Before they could record the album, Kay left the group to get married, so some rearranging of the songs was needed before the band booked into a big studio in London. It took about a week to record. Time constraints meant that a lot of it had to be recorded in one take.

The sleeve stated that it was produced by their manager Patrick Meehan Junior. In his interview Clive says that he was merely the figurehead. The engineer was Roy Thomas Baker who later went on to produce Queen and a host of other best-selling albums. Much of the album's success was down to his skill.

The album was released in March 1970 and almost made the UK top 30, peaking at number 32. It was also released in the US, Japan, Australia and Europe. The band played the 1970 Plumpton and Isle of Wight festivals.

Note the spelling of Kris Kristofferson's name on the Thursday lineup.

They were managed by Worldwide Artiste Management who also handled Black Sabbath and the occult connection was picked up by the press. While it's true that any publicity is good publicity, the group's act contained a lot of satanic ritual and the resulting hoo-hah meant they never appeared on the BBC. The proposed US tour was cancelled following the Manson murders, but they toured Europe many times.

Their record company CBS virtually ignored them, only releasing a couple of tracks on a sampler LP. Their second LP suffered from poor production and even poorer publicity. Some members wanted to drop the black magic and concentrate on the music and that caused the band to split.

After another album, unimaginatively titled Black Widow 3 flopped they were dropped by the record company.

In 1972 the remaining members regrouped and went into Derek's Beck Studio in Wellingborough to record demos for a projected fourth album. The 1972 acetate disc joined the original 1969 demo acetate underneath Clive's bed where it remained until the late 1990s when Mystic Records released it on CD as Black Widow IV.

Black Widow IV   MYS CD 117

1. SLEIGHRIDE (Trevor–Taylor–Griffith–Culley–Jones)   9.09
2. MORE THAN A DAY (Trevor–Jones)   4.29
3. YOU'RE SO WRONG (Griffith–Jones)   3.51
4. THE WAVES (Jones)   5.44
5. PART OF A NEW DAY (Trevor–Taylor–Griffith–Culley–Jones)   8.29
6. WHEN WILL YOU KNOW (Griffith–Jones)   2.23
7. FLOATING (Griffith–Jones)   4.26
8. PICTURES IN MY HEAD (Jones–Culley)   3.40
9. I SEE YOU (Griffith)   3.10
                                          Total Playing Time 45.38

Recorded and Produced by Black Widow at D.T. Studios, Kettering, Northants between August and December 1972

KIP TREVOR   –   Lead Vocals (Tracks 1-5)
CLIVE JONES   –   Flute, Saxophone & Percussion
GEOFF GRIFFITH   –   Bass Guitar & Vocals
ZOOT TAYLOR   –   Organ
ROMEO CHALLENGER   –   Drums
JOHN CULLEY   –   Lead Guitar & Vocals
RICK E   –   Lead Vocals (Tracks 6-9)

The Beck sessions were released on CD by Mystic Records.

In 1972 the band's drummer was future Showwaddywaddy member Romeo Challenger.

In 1998 the original 1969 Shield acetate was remastered and released on CD by Mystic Records and on vinyl LP by Italian label Black Widow. Reviews were very positive, considering the age of the acetate and the fact it was recorded as a demo.

The 1998 release of the Shield recording session.

The American Allmusic.com website published this review by Dave Thompson. He wrote:

'Cut while the group was still known as Pesky Gee! and working toward the follow-up to its Exclamation Mark debut, it features additional vocalist Kay Garrett alongside the familiar Kip Trevor.

While the lyrics and arrangements are unchanged, there's an urgency to this performance that the original simply cannot match.

Added emphasis on sax and organ pushes things hard, while every song is taken just a few beats faster than listeners are accustomed to, to bring a delirium to the performance that is perfectly in keeping with the subject matter. Not even the presence of a little surface noise (the CD was mastered from the acetate) can detract from the magnificence of the performance and, if you've spent the last however many years marvelling at the Sacrifice that fans know and love, this one will take you even higher.'

johnkatsmc5.blogspot.com/2017/08/black-widow-return-to-sabbat-1999.html is a page devoted to reviews of the 1998 album. Here are some excerpts:

'This was a total surprise to me! All old versions of the songs on this one are far better than on the 'Sacrifice' album! Kay's vocals bring a strange and wonderful extra element to this music, and it's sad that they didn't continue doing material with the same line-up. I first thought this was a four-star album, but careful listening cleared it out that this is truly a unique masterpiece, and it deserves five stars. The only album by this band you seriously need!' (by Eetu Pellonpaa).

'I've always previously found Black Widow to be an album I just didn't 'get', but these original demo tapes for Black Widow's debut album have won me over. With Kay Garret - lead vocalist from the band's previous incarnation as Pesky Gee - still around to provide female vocals, the theatrical intention of the conceptual song sequence is teased out more effectively (it really does help to have different people singing the different parts in this case), and whilst the sound quality isn't pristine, it's actually pretty solid for 1960s demo material. If nothing else, I can see why the likes of Blood Ceremony look to Black Widow for inspiration, and it's inspired me to take another look at their discography.' (by Warthur).

'This album is for fans only but it is still a good one (Sacrifice is just phenomenal). I would just recommend more the official release from 1970 to any proghead willing to discover this almost anonymous band. Black Widow deserves it. Three stars.' (by ZowieZiggy).

CHAPTER 22: NEW FORMULA

This band hailed from Corby and had several names over its lifetime. They started out in 1962 as The Cervezas and early gigs included The Gaiety in Ramsey when they supported a band called The Chequers on May 12th. When they returned on August 11th they were billed as Mike Harper and Cervezas. They also supported Corby band The Crusaders on October 13th. They turned professional in July 1963.

From the outset their leader Kru Zakks insisted that they were a Corby rather than a London group. They were signed to a big London Agency and changed their name to Formula Five between a short tour of Scotland and a month-long trip to Germany. The German dates really knocked them into shape. Lead singer Mick Harper said that if any band thought they were good before going out there, they'd be a hundred times better when they returned. (As recounted in Clive Smith and David Black's excellent book 'It's Steel Rock & Roll to Me.')

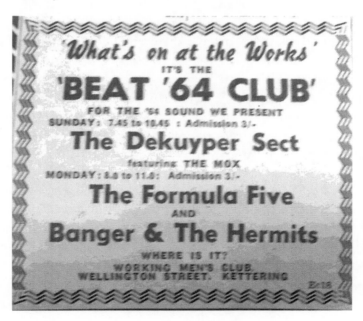

By 1964 it was becoming almost a requirement for groups to write their own songs and the band got composing.

In August they entered a beat music competition singing their own songs and made it through to the National final, finishing third overall but without breaking through to the big time.

Ringo Starr judges the National Beat Group Competition

📅 Sunday 27 September 1964   🏷 Television   💬 No Comments

Ringo Starr appeared on a judging panel for the final of the National Beat Group Competition on this day at the Prince of Wales Theatre in London.

The acts taking part, winners of previous regional heats, were The Southerns, The Connoisseurs, The Starfires, The Apaches, Formula Five, The Down-Beats, The Vibros, The Countdowns, Roy Stuart and the Cyclones, Danny Clarke and the Jaguars, and The Crusades. None achieved notability beyond this night.

Picture from Clive Smith's collection.

More European tours followed including tours of US airbases in Germany & Spain. In June 1965 the band dropped the 'Five' from their name, just prior to the release of their first single 'Close to Me', written by Tony Macaulay. It failed to set the charts alight, in part due to the band's inexperience in the studio and because they weren't in the UK to promote it.

After recording further demos at Shield, they won a recording contract with Pye early in 1966. The new single was written by Les Vandyke and recorded without the band, just Mick and an eighteen-piece orchestra.

Unfortunately, the producer didn't like the band's name and their single was released as Corby and The Champagne.

It hardly mattered because it never troubled the charts. The flip side was an original band composition. Was this the song they'd demoed at Shield?

Early in 1966 their agent booked them to play a nightly 40-minute cabaret spot in a hotel in Accra, the capital of Ghana. Derek designed and built them a new PA which they had shipped over. They loved the sound and became virtual ambassadors for Shield amplification. Many bands including The Endevers and The Fireflies bought their own systems after hearing the quality of the band's harmonies through the PA.

While they were in Accra there was a military coup and the president was overthrown. It was a scary time for the group.

The band eventually made it back to the UK by way of Liberia but without sax player Kru Zakks or their equipment.

They moped around for a couple of weeks before getting back together. Saxophonist Ricky Dodd replaced Kru and they set to work to regain lost ground. When they discovered that their band name was owned by Kru they changed their name yet again and became the New Formula. A friend at Lakenheath US airbase lent them the money to buy a cheap van and Derek built them a new PA.

They went back to playing the US bases. One night they met Alex Jack of Ajax Entertainment who was impressed enough to buy them out from their contract with the agent who had fixed up the Africa deal.

Postcard from Ghana 1966. (From Mavis' scrapbook.)

He then found them a flat in North London which became their base. His connections with the London scene meant they had residencies at many of the top clubs.

The money wasn't great but the exposure and prestige was invaluable. Their airbase contacts kept them right up to date with the latest US hits although their repertoire still included their versions of 'Maria' and 'Tonight' from West Side Story, by then almost ten years old. It was as if they were stuck in a time warp with the music scene changing almost daily around them.

In March 1967 they got a write up in the Melody Maker's 'Caught in the Act' column.

'It's always pleasant to come across a group that exudes talent, musicianship and that has made an obvious effort to get away from the usual stereotyped group sound. Such a group is the New Formula, which appeared at the Cromwellian last week.

(Mick) Harper is a good singer who can handle material ranging from Wilson Pickett's 'Funky Broadway' to things like 'Maria' and 'Tonight' which are given original treatment. Part of the joy of this group is their excellent sound system which made their songs entertaining listening. The New Formula are a group worth watching.'

Their next single was a cover of Jon & Robin's US hit song 'Do it again a little bit slower'. It did nothing in the UK but made the German Top Twenty.

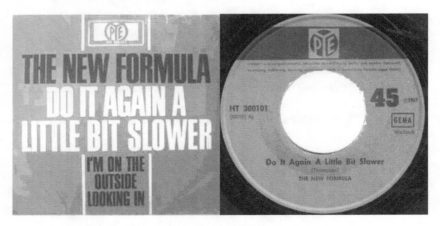

The UK release was on the Piccadilly label. This is the German version.

On July 22nd, 1967 the group performed their single on the German TV's Beat Club programme. They were introduced by Radio DJ Dave Lee Travis with a ridiculous 'Ve haff veys' English accent. The clip can be found on YouTube.

The follow up 'I Want to Go Back There Again / Can't You See That She Loves You' was another flop.

In 1968 the band released another single on the Pye label. This time the record company promoted them with some adverts in the music press and secured them a couple of appearances on prime-time TV. They continued to play the London clubs.

On February 26th they played top London night club venue Hatchetts Playground and in May they had another residency at the exclusive Cromwellian Club in South Kensington. The band was kept busy travelling the length and breadth of the country, and recording sessions for the BBC to be broadcast on the afternoon radio shows. They also began to play cabaret, a week at a time in the northern clubs.

THE NEW FORMULA TO GO ON TV AGAIN

CORBY POP group The New Formula make their second television appearance in a week, when they appear on "Time for Blackburn" on Saturday night.

Last weekend they were on the Simon Dee show and now they face the cameras again on disc jockey Tony Blackburn's show.

The group are making a big impression with their new disc "My Baby's Coming Home", which was written for them by the top team of Tony Macauley and John McLeod, who were responsible for hits by Long John Baldry, The Foundations and the Paper Dolls.

Nationally the record is moving towards the charts and is enjoying a very successful run in Corby's own hit lists.

So, what on earth convinced their agent to take a booking for the Woburn Music Festival, held that July? Not a lot of people know it, but this festival predated both the Woodstock and Isle of Wight festivals.

The New Formula opening the show for Jimi Hendrix July 1968.

Some group members were all too aware of the changing music scene and wanted to update the set. This came to a head when Mick Harper wanted to start their set with 'Maria'. A festival goer wrote this on the UK Festivals website:

New Formula! What the ...who the hell are these guys? Well, from memory they were a bleeding awful sweet soul group and NOBODY liked them. You have to feel sorry for this band, they were given an awful reception. Slow hand clap, whistles, shouts of piss off. I have a vivid memory of some tousle haired Marc Bolan clones down the front throwing toilet rolls at the lead singer, and after a while the band retired hurt. So much for the generation of love.

Band member Bruce Carey was interviewed by Clive Smith a couple of years ago. He remembers the day well:

'We had an argument about our set list in which Mick insisted we started with PJ Proby's 'Maria'. Great song but not exactly what the long-haired flower dripping acid headed youth wanted! It didn't take long before the jeering started, followed by coke cans and rubbish being hurled at us on stage. That had never happened before - we always went down well. It was the start of Underground or Progressive music, soul music wasn't the coolest anymore.'

Later that summer Mavis and Derek were about to sit down to dinner when they had a phone call from the band. One of their amplifiers had stopped working and they were due to play a big booking at a top Sheffield hotel. Derek took a new amp from stock and he and Mavis drove to the venue, handed the amplifier over and stayed to watch the band perform to a packed room.

On Oct 22nd Derek and John Dobson's Shield Electronics firm had a stand at a trade show at the Halfway House Hotel in Luton. As well as the usual displays of amplifiers and speaker cabinets Derek had arranged for both The New Formula and Steve Fearn's Brass Foundry to entertain the packed room and to demonstrate the quality of the amplification they were selling.

Mavis remembers it well. She said that Derek had it all planned but forgot to invite her! It didn't help that John's wife Sue was going and even had an I.D. Badge and that made Mavis angry. Derek said she could go as long as she got a lift. In the end Sue took her. It was her first time on the M1, and she did ninety miles an hour all the way. Mavis' comment was short and to the point:

'Bloody show-off!'

Christmas Eve 1968.

The Evening Telegraph February 1969.

Early in 1969 Scottish singer Lulu had a Saturday night prime time show on BBC1 TV as a prelude to that year's Eurovision Song Contest (which she won with 'Boom Bang A Bang'.) The New Formula appeared on the February 8th programme. Mavis said that they mimed to a track that was recorded at Shield, a cover version of the 5th Dimension's hit 'Up Up And Away'.

Despite all the publicity the breakthrough into the big time never happened.

Mavis was a big fan of the band. She says that Mick Harper's rendition of the West Side Story song 'Maria' was absolutely first class. It's very clear from listening to their records that his voice was something special. The big stage hit of 1969 was the 'Hair' musical and the band released their version of 'Hare Krishna' in August. Alas, it was not to be. George Harrison and the Radna-Krishna Temple's single with the same name was released at the same time. The tensions within the band were such that Mick was eventually asked to leave and was replaced by Eddie Ayres.

Released in 1969.

When Kru reappeared on the scene he had reinvented himself as a DJ. Derek supplied him with a brand-new Shield double deck, amplifier and speaker set-up. Mavis is unsure if they were ever paid for. She thinks he moved to the South Coast soon afterwards. When he was last heard of in 1997 he was living back in his native Latvia.

Kru Zakks and Shield disco decks (from Mavis' scrapbook).

CHAPTER 23: JOHN DEACON & THE OPPOSITION/ART

June 22nd, 1968. Leicester band Art supporting Honeybus.

Art featuring 17-year-old future Queen bass player John Deacon played the Tin Hat in June 1968. The band had begun as The Opposition about three years earlier and it's unclear exactly when or why they changed their name. John was only 14 when he joined the group. In an article published in the February 1996 issue of Record Collector, John's former bandmates talked about their early days, when their ambitions stretched no further than the next booking, probably somewhere deep in the Leicestershire countryside. According to band member Richard Young, Deacon was possibly the least ambitious member of the group.

Whether by accident or design, the group got a booking supporting Honeybus at the Tin Hat. Sometime in the next few months they went into Derek's studio to record a couple of tracks.

It wasn't the first or last time that a group played at the Tin Hat and then recorded at Shield. Was someone having a quiet word in their ears?

In the article band member Nigel Bullen said that there wasn't any reasoning behind the demo. They just fancied recording a couple of numbers. When they arrived at the studio, they were told that they had time to record three songs, which was awkward because they'd only prepared two. The third track was a hastily composed tune about their latest van. It was called 'Transit 3' and was the first and possibly only original song they wrote together. One of them remembers that the room had nice acoustics and that the guy (Derek) knew what he was doing.

John Deacon left the group in June 1969 to study electronics at Chelsea College of Science & Technology. (Roger Kinsey graduated from there in June 1967.) He played one solitary gig in November 1970. The band was called Deacon and they supported Hardin York, another group that recorded at Shield and Beck. The third band Idle Race was fronted by Jeff Lynne who later teamed up with Roy Wood to form the Electric Light Orchestra.

John Deacon joined Queen in 1971 and as they say, the rest is history.

And it all began with Derek Tompkins at Shield.

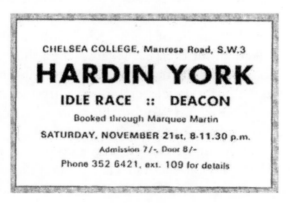

CHELSEA COLLEGE, Manresa Road, S.W.3

HARDIN YORK

IDLE RACE :: DEACON

Booked through Marquee Martin

SATURDAY, NOVEMBER 21st, 8-11.30 p.m.

Admission 7/-, Door 8/-

Phone 352 6421, ext. 109 for details

CHAPTER 24: 1969

1969 was a fitting end to the sixties. Back in 1961 JFK gave a speech to Congress where he set out the goal of landing a man on the moon and returning him safely to the earth by the end of the decade. On July 21st over 500 million people around the world tuned in to see Neil Armstrong step down the ladder and utter those immortal words: 'One small step for man-

Northamptonshire

Evening Telegraph

CLOSE-UP ON THE MOON WALK – CENTRE PAGES

A giant leap for mankind

Monday, July 21, 1969   5d

On the music front the New Year began on January 12th with the US release of Led Zeppelin's first LP. Less than three weeks later The Beatles give their last ever public performance on the roof of their Savile Row headquarters.

Early in the year two iconic passenger aircraft made their maiden flights. February 9th saw the Boeing 747, forever known as the jumbo jet take off from the Boeing airfield at Everett, Washington. Less than a month later on March 2nd the Anglo/French supersonic passenger jet Concorde flew for the first time.

John Lennon married Yoko One in Gibraltar on March 20th and held their honeymoon 'Bed-In' in a hotel in Amsterdam.

Lulu was pronounced the joint winner of that year's Eurovision Song Contest held in Madrid. Four countries tied on 18 points each and the rules were hastily changed to prevent a recurrence.

In April British troops were deployed in Ulster to support the local constabulary and remained throughout the Troubles, only leaving for good in 2007.

Eric Clapton and Steve Winwood started jamming together following the breakup of Cream and Traffic.

They were soon joined by drummer Ginger Baker and decided to form a group. Family's bass player Rik Grech completed the lineup. They called themselves Blind Faith and promptly rented a cottage in the country in order to 'get it together man', before releasing their debut album complete with a topless picture of a prepubescent girl holding a phallic looking model of a plane on the cover. Not surprisingly the cover was changed for the US release. The album only lacked one thing- some decent songs. They played one free show in Hyde Park, toured the US and then split up. Did the public believe the 'supergroup' hype and expect too much of them?

These iconic aircraft made their maiden flights in 1969.

On July 3rd ex-Rolling Stones guitarist Brian Jones was found at the bottom of his swimming pool, just a couple of days before the group played their first live show in over a year in front of a huge crowd in Hyde Park. Estimates of the crowd size varied between a quarter and half a million people.

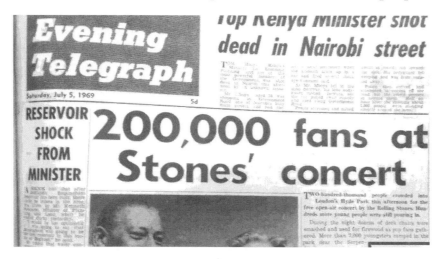

A month or so later, on August 9th the Beatles were pictured on a zebra crossing in Abbey Road by photographer Iain Macmillan and the image was used on the front cover of the album that many people think is one of their finest. The album was released at the end of September.

The onset of decimalisation.

On August 9th Charles Manson's 'family' went on the rampage in an orgy of violence at the home of actress Sharon Tate and her film director husband Roman Polanski. Tate and three of her friends were stabbed more than a hundred times.

A week or so later the Woodstock Festival was held in upstate New York. A film crew was on hand to capture the action for a documentary that was released in March 1970. They had so much footage that a split screen technique was used to show four different images at the same time. Even then the film was over three hours long.

Some acts like Joe Cocker and Ten Years After went on to global superstardom after their performances were shown in cinemas worldwide.

Many people (the author included) saw the film several times. It was strange but entirely appropriate to applaud the bands on the silver screen, especially the performance of Jimi Hendrix who died a few months after the film was released.

In October 5th the first episode of Monty Python's Flying Circus was shown on TV. Two weeks later Led Zeppelin II was released to critical acclaim and commercial success.

The Rolling Stones LP Let It Bleed was released on December 5th, just in time for Christmas. Meanwhile the band was 6000 miles away at the Altamont Speedway in northern California. Despite everyone's best intentions the weekend was best remembered for the violent scenes in front of the stage. Whatever happened to peace and love?

CHAPTER 25: TV TIMES

Television is an even more recent medium than sound recording. The British Broadcasting Corporation first started making television programmes in 1932 but regular broadcasting from Alexandra Palace didn't begin until November 1936 and was restricted to the London area. There were probably fewer than 20,000 TV sets in use when the broadcasts were suspended upon the outbreak of war. Broadcasting resumed in June 1946.

Brightest stars of television . . .
Eamonn Andrews and the NEW

G.E.C. 14 in. television

Biggest value of 1953. Large, steady, brilliant picture, handsome compact walnut veneered cabinet, remarkably low price — and G.E.C. dependability! It matters a great deal who makes your TV receiver. You can trust the G.E.C.! These famous initials never appear on any model till it has been tested in the laboratory, in production, and *at work in all TV areas.* Write for fully descriptive publication BT 2073, and the name of your nearest G.E.C. approved dealer to *The General Electric Co. Ltd.,* (*B10*) *Magnet House, Kingsway, W.C.2.*

★ New filter-faced, long-life tube gives full daylight viewing, eliminates halation and renders a separate filter unnecessary.

★ Barretter current control protects the tube and valves from harm due to fluctuating electricity mains supply.

★ Brightest, clearest and largest 14 inch picture.

BT 5147

60

GNS tax paid
or hire purchase

The BBC opened a transmitter covering the Midlands just before Christmas 1949 and gradually the TV set became the focus of attention in living rooms across the country. The sets were very expensive and within a couple of years TV rental became the preferred option for many people.

Rent your Television

You can enjoy trouble-free television for a modest rental which covers all repairs and replacements, including valves and tube. What's more, you can change to a new model any time

Models from

10/- reducing to

8/- weekly

Initial Payment 50 - Aerial extra

Call in our showroom for demonstration, or send for our leaflet

Rentaset

RADIO AND TELEVISION HIRE SERVICE

The live broadcast of the Coronation in June 1953 prompted a huge increase in the number of sets in the UK. Derek was working as a TV repairman, first of all at the Co-op in Montagu Street and later at George Reader's in Gordon Street. His time in the REME working on radar sets had come in very useful and he soon gained a reputation for the quality of his work.

When Commercial TV began broadcasting in 1955 the TVs needed to be converted to receive the new channel, or one could upgrade to a two-channel set like this Bush model.

£54 guineas was a lot of money when beer was about a shilling (5p) a pint!

ITV used a different transmitter, so it meant a more complicated aerial was needed. Soon the town's rooftops and chimneys were adorned with a forest of aluminium TV aerials. By the end of 1955 more than 90% of the country could receive BBC but Dave remembers that it was 1959 before Westward TV began broadcasting to his hometown in Cornwall.

A typical 1950s roofscape with TV aerials.

By the late 1950s Derek was ready to open his own business and he and Mavis found a shop with upstairs living accommodation in Regent Street, just off the Rockingham Road. They offered a TV and electrical repair service and sold top end hi-fi equipment including tape recorders.

The Consumers Association launched their annual 'Which?' magazine in October 1957. One of their early issues featured this guide to purchasing a television set:

'Which? is publishing this week the results of tests on 17in table models, with descriptions of the brands which give the best picture and the best sound. There appears to be a closer correlation between price and quality in TV sets than in most of the other goods with which we have dealt so far. Reliability, however, is far more difficult to assess than quality of sound or picture. It varies not only between brands but between different models made by the same firm and different samples of the same model.

Most shopkeepers handle only a few brands. Buy from one of the firms' appointed agents. He may not be the most distinguished retailer in the district, but he will know most about the foibles of the set you want.

Do not, obviously, buy the set which has been switched on in the window for the past month, entertaining the neighbourhood. It will be virtually second-hand. Do not, on the other hand, insist on a crated, sealed set delivered on your doorstep. This would mean that the retailer's service engineer had had no chance to check and adjust it. The best plan, if you have the nerve, is to get the retailer to open a sealed crate in the shop, note the serial number of the set from the back panel and check you have the same set when it is installed in your house.

Make sure before you buy that the man who is selling you the set is interested in installing it properly. Then, later on, it will be serviced properly. But the buyer has to give time and interest also. Half an hour on a Saturday morning cannot be expected to get good results for anyone.

A television should last for five to seven years, but not without trouble. The best person for the servicing is usually the original retailer, changed (to another agent of the maker) if he is not quick, efficient and cheap.

Valves are guaranteed for three months, tubes for a year. New tubes cost £10-£15, re-gunned ones £5-£10, plus installation charges. Re-gunned tubes have been on the market for too short a time to generalise about their length of life. Servicing charges are about 13 shillings an hour for the engineer's time. Always ask for an itemised bill and expect to pay £30 to £60 in service and replacement charges over five to seven years.

Consider a contract maintenance scheme. They sometimes have varying premiums – more as the sets get older. Most average about £8 a year. If the set lasted for five years, this would be £40 – ie less than you would pay otherwise if you were unlucky with your set, more than if you were lucky. Telesurance Ltd has a similar scheme.

Many firms rent sets and two– Radio Rentals and Domestic Electric Rentals (D·E·R) operate all over the country. With these, it costs roughly £100-£110 to rent for five years and you get free servicing. If you buy a set which lasts for five years, renting and buying cost about the same. If your set lasts for seven years, renting costs more.

As regards the appearance of the set, out of some 30 firms making televisions, only seven feature in the Council of Industrial Design's Design Index. Since they are an essential piece of the living-room furniture in so many of our homes, this seems a little sad.'

(The average working man's wage in 1960 was about £14 a week (£700 pa) and the £100 referred to in the article would be almost £2000 now)

The first sets used the VHF (Very High Frequency) 405-line standard that had been adopted by the government at the end of the war. This was replaced by the UHF (Ultra High Frequency) 625-line TV standard in 1964 when BBC2 was launched. Of course, a new aerial was needed, and reception was a bit iffy due to the poor tuners in the sets. It was almost fifteen years before UHF was available to 90% of the country. Some sets were equipped to operate on both 405 and 625 but switching from one to the other via a big knob on the side of the set caused the picture to flicker and crackle ominously. It wasn't long before the BBC and ITV began broadcasting their shows on both 405 and 625 systems and one less risk of a catastrophic failure of the TV set was averted.

BBC2 began broadcasting in colour in 1967, with ITV and BBC1 following a couple of years later. Colour TV licences were introduced on 1st January 1968 and cost £10, which was twice the price of the standard £5 black and white TV licence. Other notable events during the 60s included the first transatlantic broadcast via the Telstar satellite, (spawning a worldwide hit for the Joe Meek produced tune 'Telstar' by The Tornados. It was a number 1 in the UK, US, Belgium, Ireland and South African charts.)

On the 25th June 1967 a world-wide satellite TV programme called 'Our World' was broadcast live to an international audience of about 400 million. The UK's contribution featured The Beatles performing 'All You Need Is Love' in a crowded Studio Two at Abbey Road Studios. The band performed to a backing track with Lennon singing live. Part of the backing was recorded at Olympic Sound Studio in Barnes before being mixed down to a mono track that was added to the mix along with a string section back at Abbey Road. There was a 13-piece orchestra in the studio for the broadcast and a host of friends, including The Rolling Stones, Eric Clapton, Marianne Faithfull and Graham Nash joined in the chorus and added to the atmosphere. When the single was released in July it topped the charts in almost every country in the world.

On 23rd August 1968 Barry Noble, backed by Steve Fearn's Brass Foundry starred in an episode of BBC2's Colour Me Pop. Unfortunately, the BBC destroyed the video and only the audio has survived.

July 1969 saw two more events that attracted world wide audiences. On the 1st the Investiture of Prince Charles at Caernarfon Castle was shown live on TV, followed three weeks later when over half a billion people tuned in to watch Neil Armstrong step on to the surface of the moon.

Derek's TV repair business may not have been the most spectacular or high-profile part of what he did, but it was an ever-constant occupation through such a momentous decade of change. It's also true that some of his working practices would fail modern Health & Safety standards. A lifetime of working with electricity had left him almost immune from shocks. Steve Fearn remembers that if an amplifier or other electronic kit needed working on, he wouldn't bother switching it off but would dive right in, ignoring the sparks and electric shocks. Mavis said that he often worked with the back of the TV set open with all the electrics exposed. He used to lean over the set to see the TV screen in order to see the results of his adjustments. On one occasion the metal zip on his trousers touched a live wire inside the TV set. He soon discovered that it was only his hands that were impervious to pain!

CHAPTER 26: STUDIO SUCCESS

In 1968 Shield Electronics were going from strength to strength. Orders were coming from far and near for their sound systems. Derek was helped at the Cambridge Street factory by Mavis' brother Alan who wired up the amplifiers while John split his time between working at the factory, getting orders and looking after the admin side of the business.

Mavis kept some letters in her scrapbook including this one from the manager of O'Hara's Playboys. They had seen and heard the New Formula's PA and wanted their own setup.

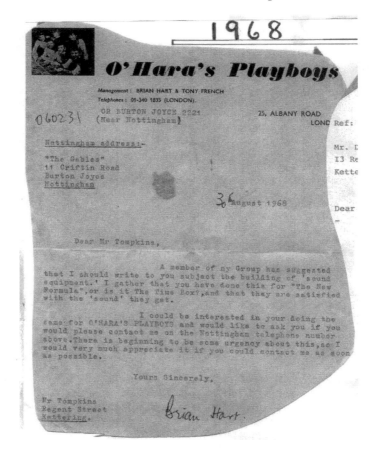

30th August 1968

'Dear Mr Tompkins,

A member of my Group has suggested that I should write to you subject to the building of 'sound equipment'. I gather that you have done this for 'The New Formula', or is it The Time Box? (It was both groups), and that they are satisfied with the 'sound' they get.

I could be interested in your doing the same for O'HARA'S PLAYBOYS and would like to ask you if you would please contact me on the Nottingham telephone number above. There is beginning to be some urgency about this, so I would very much appreciate it is you could contact me as soon as possible.

Yours Sincerely, Brian Hart.

The article in the Evening Telegraph back in August 1968 had been good for business. The studio (which was a separate business to the amplification side) was as busy as ever. Jimmy James and The Vagabonds with their new keyboard player Bill Coleman called in early in December 1968. Derek was so confident about the studio's future that on December 6th he bought a disc cutting lathe. The first acetate was cut for Jimmy James the following day.

Bill Coleman's copy of Jimmy James & the Vagabonds' acetate.

Some of the bands that recorded at Shield in 1969 included:

Feb 18th   The Loving Kind (with Steve Fearn).
March 7th   Steve Fearn records new song 'It's too late'.
March 7th   Corby band The Carnations record at Shield.
(evening)

The Carnations 1969.

On March 19th Derek went down to London with The Carnations for a Radio 1 Club recording session.

Two days earlier Timebox were in the studio to record 'Baked Jam Roll in your Eye' and acetate discs were cut. Deram Records released the song a little later in the year. It's not clear if they used the Shield recording.

As already mentioned, both Whitesnake's Bernie Marsden and Queen's John Deacon recorded tracks that year.

According to Steve Fearn, the first group to have a Shield recording released as a single was Leicester based Mint. They are also the only act to have won TV talent shows Opportunity Knocks and New Faces and were a hugely successful act on the Talk of the Town and Baileys club circuit during the 1970s.

Mint.

Luv was written to promote a Lyons Maid ice lolly of the same name that was launched in the UK on the 12th of May 1969. The television advert featured a pre-Space Oddity David Bowie singing along on the Luv, Luv, Luv chorus.

Timebox was originally formed in Southport, Lancashire in 1965 and moved down to London. It's unclear exactly how they came to use a Shield PA or record at Shield, but they became good friends with Derek and Mavis.

On March 22nd 8-piece soul band Hal C Blake recorded at Shield. The following day was folk singer Phil Downer's turn.

On Mar 26th Derek went to London with Barry Noble to record a BBC Radio1 show.

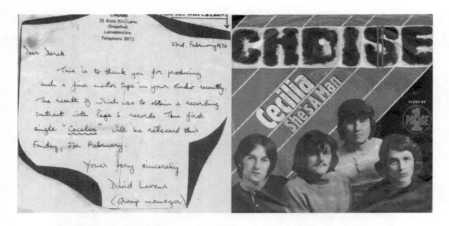

Recorded at Shield. Released in February 1970 on Page1 Records.

During the summer term some pupils from Kettering Grammar School paid a visit to the studio to see how it worked. Keith Sheffield says that he was the first to put his hand up- anything to get out of algebra lessons! A few weeks later he went back to ask if there were any jobs going. Derek agreed to take him on as he was about to set up a new venture in Wellingborough- Beck Studios. Keith's story will be told in the next book.

Other pupils on the visit included guitarists Max Norman and Ian Hunt. Eddie Giacobbe remembers that he, Ian and Max used to jam together in Max's mum's front room. Max was in his early teens and was already making his name as a guitarist in local bands. He was one of the first in Kettering to own a Gibson Les Paul (a 1959 two pickup double cutaway TV model). He had his guitar with him and was able to record a short rhythm guitar part and overlaid it with a guitar solo. It was his first experience of being in a studio. Soon afterwards his guitar neck was broken due an unfortunate mishap and he switched to a newer single cutaway model.

In 1972 drummer Mick Austin and Max Norman's band Land played a support spot at London's Marquee Club.

A couple of years later Max was running the live sound for bands including Uriah Heep and Motörhead and by the end of the 70s he was resident sound engineer at Ridge Farm Studio in Surrey.

In 1980 he took over from Chris Tsangarides as producer of Ozzy Osbourne's Blizzard of Oz album. It became a worldwide hit and within a year or two Max was in demand as one of the world's top producers of heavy metal music.

And it all began with Derek Tompkins at Shield.

Land's reunion in 2019. Max Norman is on the right next to Mick Austin.
Former roadies Neil & Dennis in the background.

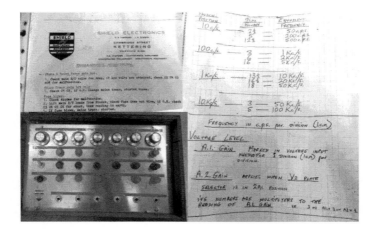

Pete Grantham's Shield User's Manual was handwritten by Derek.

Derek continued to manage the Q Men, while Mavis looked after the bookings. Des Leonard had taken over from Mike Benford on lead vocals.

Des recalls that The Q Men played at a gig in a Nottingham dance hall where they were supporting a well known 20 piece dance band. About a week later Barry Hart suddenly dropped a bombshell, saying that he'd been invited to join the band. They had two weeks to find a replacement. By a stroke of good fortune Barri Michael Jones had just moved from Wales to Corby and saw the advert. Des went to see him at his home. He said 'As soon as he picked up his guitar and started singing I knew we had hit the jackpot, he was brilliant.'

Barri Jones' first gig with the band was at the agricultural College in Sawtry before Barry Hart left. Barri's first show after taking over lead guitar was in a huge marquee at Bourne Lincs where they were the support band for The Love Affair. Barry Hart was back within a month, having had some sort of fall out with the dance band leader. Alas, the Q Men were happy with his replacement so he eventually moved to the US with his wife Carol.

CHAPTER 27: THE BREAKUP

It was 1969. The October 1968 trade show had been a great success. The former Maple Ballroom in Bridge Street Northampton changed to Shades Disco early in 1969 and Shield supplied all the disco and amplification equipment. They also had a lot of publicity after they installed a complete system in Rushden's Windmill Club.

Shield Electronics had a full order book, so it came as a great shock to be told by Mavis' father that the company was over £3000 overdrawn at the bank (about the price of a brand new semi-detached house in Kettering) and he was unwilling to put in any more money. So where had the money gone?

John was responsible for the sales side of the business. Derek told him that the number of non-paying customers was clear evidence that he wasn't pulling his weight. Relations between John and Derek swiftly deteriorated. On January 25th, 1969 Derek told Mavis' father that he was dissolving the partnership and setting up on his own. The whole break up left Derek and Mavis battered and bruised both mentally and physically.

More was to come. The Tin Hat had always had its fair share of boisterous clientele and the bouncers were always kept busy. Things came to a head in February when the appearance by Plastic Penny ended in uproar. Brian's wife Mavis had to go the local police station in order to identify the culprits and a few days later Derek decided that working behind the bar every Saturday night following a busy day in the studio was only adding to his troubles. He handed in his notice on the tenth. By the end of the month the venue had changed hands. Both Brian Tompkins and Alan Dobson started appearing at other venues and they were no longer advertised on the Tin Hat dates.

Apart from the aforementioned appearance by Plastic Penny on February 1st and Status Quo on May 3rd the artists booked through 1969 were largely lesser known.

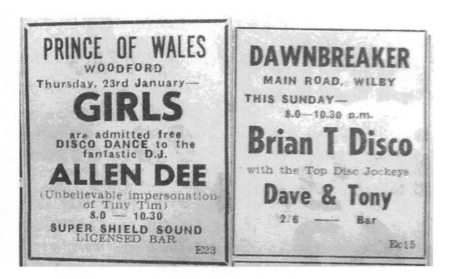

January and February 1969 dates.

During May 1969 Derek was asked to record some school choirs in Wellingborough. The sessions were very tightly timed in order to fit in with the school day and it was all too often a rush to get in and set up in the time available. Di Evans remembers when Derek came to her school to record an LP. She says that he was a lovely man.

At the end of June, a request came in to record several schools in the Morecambe area. He enlisted Mavis as his roadie and assistant and Mavis' parents looked after Lynda. They loaded up the van with the recording equipment and set off. When they arrived it was pouring with rain, but they found a B&B and spent the rest of the day recording two school choirs. The evening was spent in a deserted nightclub where Mavis was serenaded by the cabaret singer. The next two days were wet and miserable, but Derek was kept busy recording at least two school choirs per day.

On the evening of the first of July, they went to a local pub to watch the highlights of Prince Charles' Investiture as Prince of Wales on the pub's colour TV but were refused admission because women weren't allowed in the bar.

They returned home after recording seven school choirs. Mavis said that the money wasn't much to write home about but both Derek's and the studio's reputations were given a well-deserved boost. After a week of humping gear and struggling with microphones, stands and leads Mavis concluded that a roadie's life wasn't for her. Towards the end of June Derek formally told Mavis' father and her brother John that he was leaving.

Meanwhile their TV shop had several customers with long outstanding bills which added to their money worries. At least the recording studio was doing well and making money.

The partnership was finally dissolved at the end of July. It soon became apparent that without Derek's input Shield Electronics was doomed, and so it proved to be. On August 23rd Derek asked Mavis to look for a suitable house with room for a shop and recording studio, and they cleared out the garden shed and began accumulating woodworking and other tools. He would continue to record at Shield for the time being.

Almost the final group to record at Shield Studio was a Leicester band called Pesky Gee! After their debut album on the Pye label flopped they decided on a change of direction, a change of name and an album of original material based on the then current interest in the occult. They spent most of September in the studio and emerged with a fully mastered long-playing record and a new name- Black Widow. As previously recounted, Saturday September 27th was the day that Bernie Marsden and his group Skinny Cat recorded at Shield for the first time.

It had taken six months to complete the breakup of the business. The breakdown in the personal relationships took a lot longer to heal, but it was time to look forward to the future, not dwell on the past.

Finally, in August 1969 a ray of light broke through the gloom. Vic White & John Douglas booked a session at Shield and during the day said that they were interested in setting up a recording studio in Wellingborough. Vic's father owned a fruit & vegetable wholesale business in Gisburne Road. There was an empty building on the site. Derek stopped working for Shield in order to concentrate on the new venture.

Within a few days they had set up in partnership and applied for planning permission to convert the premises to a factory to manufacture Derek's new range of amplification along with a recording studio. Planning permission was granted in November and the builders moved in.

Beck Sound and Beck Recording Studio were about to take off.

This advert was run for a week in September 1969.
Once Beck was up and running the business folded.

EPILOGUE: RIP ALAN DOBSON

Mavis' younger brother Alan had been ill for some time while we were writing this book and we never had a chance to interview him. He died on April 13th, 2020, a day before Mavis' birthday. His son had the task of clearing the contents of his home in Cambridge Street, next door to the house containing the factory office. It took some time to clear the property because Alan was a compulsive hoarder.

On Thursday May 14th Dave had a message from guitarist Derrick Clements who lived opposite Alan and had known him for many years. The final skips were about to be taken away and there were three old Shield amplifiers about to be dumped. He rushed around as quickly as he could but alas, it was too late. The amplifiers were buried deep in the skip. At least Derrick had taken a photo. The top one appears to be a late model four channel PA, the middle one looks like a stereo disco amplifier and the bottom one may be another PA amplifier. Alan was an integral part of the Derek Tompkins story and he will be much missed.

A lifetime of personal effects and memories taken away by skip.

END OF PART ONE

ABOUT THE AUTHORS

Dave Clemo was born in Cornwall almost exactly in the middle of the last century. His family moved to London in 1962. He started playing guitar in the mid 60s and spent the next fifty years untroubled by success, fame and riches. Over the years he has played almost every style of music from rock to pop, folk to country, punk, funk and gospel music in every kind of venue from big theatres to festival stages, churches, pubs, clubs and house concerts.

He turned to writing after a series of health issues put an end to his touring days and has written six books to date. He was fortunate to have recorded at Derek Tompkins' Beck Studio in the 70s and 80s and jumped at the chance to research and co author this book with Mavis and Roger.

Roger Kinsey was born on Bastille Day, July 14th, 1945. His Peckham born mother wasn't allowed to keep him, so he was put up for adoption when he was six weeks old. His adoptive parents gave him a privileged upbringing even if neither were musically inclined. His baptism into 'Pop Music' occurred at the tender age of 9 when he saw Johnnie Ray at the London Palladium. He said it was in error, but thanks God it was!

He soon became a fan of the brand-new Rock & Roll, not to mention Jazz, Blues, Classical and many other music genres.

His passion is to ensure that 'LIVE MUSIC' in the entire sense of those two words will last forever. To that end he says:

'Recording music is vital to ensure future generations of anyone musical has a back catalogue to refer too for their own creative output. This is why I approached Mavis in 2018 to set the wheels (or should that be REELS) in motion to record Derek's commitment and professionalism in ensuring that the musicians who passed through his studio doors received the very best result he could give them. Derek was a humble man who deserves wider recognition.

He hopes that everyone will enjoy reading this first part of his story and agree with his sentiments.

Mavis Tompkins first met Derek when she was 14 and was married to him for 56 years until his death in November 2013.

She kept a diary for many of those years and drew on them when she published her autobiography 'Making the Best of It' in 2005. A lot of her photographs and mementos have been used to illustrate this book. Many of Derek's studio clients became close friends and have maintained close contact over the years. She set up many of the interviews that helped flesh out the account.

Mavis keeps active despite her advancing years and enjoys painting, writing and gardening, and visiting her daughter in the USA.

APPENDIX 1: THE TIN HAT DATES

Between 1967 and 1969 the Tin Hat was an important part of Kettering's entertainment and night life. Every weekend the venue was packed to the rafters with people out to enjoy a good time. The acts that Brian booked covered almost every genre from Blues and Prog to Soul and Pop- and even jazz for a few weeks during the summer of 1967. The club was usually open on Fridays, Saturdays and Sundays, with live bands on Saturdays. Some of the descriptions of the groups make interesting reading half a century later.

People travelled to the venue from Rothwell, Desborough and Corby and from Christmas 1967 the club laid on late buses to get everyone home. The management of the club changed hands early in 1969 and an era was at an end. The venue continued for a few more years but mainly concentrated on Soul/Motown.

Opening night Sat June 10th 1967.

Sat Jun 10th- Horatio Soul & the Square Deals Show.
plus, Yvonne the limbo dancer and the Q Men.
Sun Jun 11th- (Fontana recording artists) The Night People plus The Trax.

The Nite People open new discotheque
Teenscene by Linda Hutchins

What better way to launch a new discotheque than to book a new and promising group for the first session. Hence The Nite People's appearance when the Tin Hat in Rockingham Road, Kettering, opened on Sunday night.
When the Nite People formed in 1965 they hadn't got a clue what to call themselves. After close analysis- they stayed up half the night and slept half the morning- they decided to call themselves- The Nite People. It was a memorable day- it was April 1. In the first year they did most of the spade work for their career.
They toured Germany and Austria for four months gleaning valuable experience before returning to their homeland. In October they signed to Avenue Artistes and appointed Terry Ralph as personal manager, and followed this in November by making their first BBC Television appearance. Incidentally, in case you missed the boys on Sunday, there are five of them- Johnny Warwick, vocalist and lead guitar, Frances Gordon, bass; Christopher Ferguson, drummer; Harry Curtis, piano and organ and Patrick Bell, tenor and flute.
The boys have had the distinction of touring with the Beach Boys and with Martha and the Vandellas, both of which boosted their national popularity. As yet they have not broken into the charts- but it's not for want of trying. Twelve months ago they made an independent recording with Bob James- an original number by Kirby Small- Martha (of Vandella fame)'s guitarist. Entitled 'Sweet Tasting Wine' it sold well for a first disc. On March 17th this year they released a big soulful single 'Try to Find Another Man'- a number one hit for the Righteous Brothers in America, but that has not happened- yet! The last I heard the factory had to press a new lot of the disc to meet the demand. The Nite People are not kids- Francis is 20 and Chris is 22. The others are all 24, so they are under no illusion about overnight fame, but I feel that given time and the facilities to develop the kind of soul sound that could be among the evergreen names.

Friday June 16th- (from Coventry) Inside Out.
Sat June 17th- (from the USA) Winston G backed by The Set plus The Ironsides.
Sun June 18th- (Top surfing performers) Deuce Coupe.
Fri June 23rd- Dimples plus Updown Round Sound (Oxford).
Sat June 24th- (Surfing harmony group) The Symbols plus, The Swamp.
Sun June 25th- Gravy Train (B'Ham) plus Disco.
Fri July 1st- Discotheque.
Sat July 2nd- Sean Buckley Big Set plus Stumbling and Falling plus Rio Moody Dancers.
Sun July 3rd- (Radio TV and Recording stars) The Peeps.
Fri July 7th- Disco.
Sat July 8th- (Coloured Colourful CBS Recorders) The Gass.
Sun July 9th- Disco.
Fri July 14th- Disco.
Sat July 15th- Joyce Bond (Do the Teasy) Band Show.
Sun July 16th- Jazz Disco.
Sat July 22nd- (From London) Shell Shock Tamla Show.
Fri July 28th- Disco.
Sat July 29th- Wynder K Frog & his Frogmen plus, The Plastic Dreamboat light show.
Sat August 5th- The C.A.T. plus U.S.A. Flattop.
Sat Aug 12th- The Syn plus The Friction.

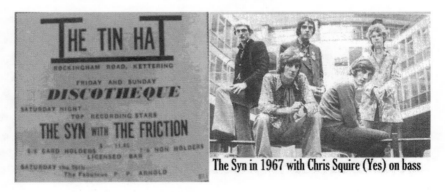

The Syn in 1967 with Chris Squire (Yes) on bass

Fri Aug 18th- Allan D Disco (Alan Dobson is Mavis' brother)
Sat Aug 19th- P P Arnold with her Nice. A few weeks later
they had split from her. Organist Keith Emerson later
became a global superstar with Emerson, Lake & Palmer.

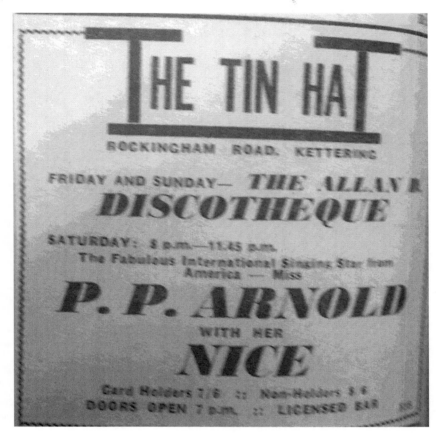

Sun Aug 20th- Disco.
Fri Aug 25th- Disco.
Sat Aug 26th- The Reg James Explosion plus Crash Landing.
Sun Aug 27th- Disco.
Fri Sep 1st- Allan D Disco.
Sat Sep 2nd- Ebony Keys with the Hip Hooray Band, plus,
The Unit Six.
Sat Sep 9th- John Mayall's Blues Breakers with support from
Pesky Gee!

Fri Sep 15th- The 'Fabulous' Temptations plus The Invaders.

The Fantastics were singers John Cheatdom, Jerome Ramos, Donald Haywoode and Richard Pitts.
They had enjoyed US chart success before being brought to the UK by promoter Roy Tempest in late 1967.
They were billed as the 'Fabulous Temptations' (despite having no connection with the more famous Motown act).
The group's debut UK tour took place in September 1967.

Sat Sep 16th- Root & Jenny Jackson with the Hightimers, plus, Purple Barrier.
Fri Sep 22nd- Deuce Coupe.
Sat Sep 23rd- Disco.
Fri Sep 29th Original Drifters. (One of Roy Tempest's fakes)
Sat Sep 30th- Freddie Mac and the Mac Sound, plus The Survivors.
Sat Oct 7th- Nite People plus Stumblin 'n Falling Blues Band.
Sun Oct 8th- Spencers Washboard Kings.
Sat Oct 14th- Disco.
Sun Oct 15th- Max Collie's Rhythm Aces.
Sat Oct 21st- Riot Squad plus the Triads.
Sun Oct 22nd- Bill Nile's Delta Jazzband.
Fri Oct 27th- Image- (Kettering's 1st and Only Light Show Scene).
Sat Oct 28th- The Gass supported by The Traxx.
Fri Nov 3rd- Disco.
Sat Nov 4th- (From Detroit) Max Baer and the Chicago Setback support by Friction.
Fri Nov 10th- Allan D Disco.
Sat Nov 11th- Mike Stuart Span supported by The Dream plus Rio Moody Style Dancers.
Sun Nov 12th- Allan D Disco.
Fri Nov 17th- Allan D Disco.
Sat Nov 18th- Rob Storme and the Whispers.
Sat Nov 25th- Family with support from Sh You Know Who.
Sat Dec 2nd- Sugar Simone and the Programm & Mo Brown and Hellions People.
Sun Dec 3rd- Allan Dee Disco.
Sat Dec 9th- Pinkertons Assorted Colours plus The Heretics.
Sun Dec 10th- Allan D Disco.
Sat Dec 16th- P.P. Arnold with the TNT, plus The Crew.
Sun Dec 17th- Allan D Disco.
Sat Dec 23rd- Shevelles plus the Kobalts.
Sun Dec 24th- Laverne West and the Fabulous Rangers Showband.
Tues Dec 26th- Swinging Q Men & the Spectre Powerhouse.

Sat Dec 30th- King Ozzie, Earl Green, Honey Darling and the Coloured Raisings Show.
Sun Dec 31st- Sweethearts & the Adlib Group.

Tin Hat Dates 1968

Sat Jan 6th- Peter Green and Fleetwood Mac plus John James and the Swamp Band (from Northampton.)
Sat Jan 13th- Amboy Dukes plus Surrealist Adventure.
Sat Jan 20th- Triads plus the Ironsides.
Sat Jan 27th- Milton James and the Harlem Knock-out, plus Sweethearts.
Sat Feb 3rd- James & Bobby Purify plus Surrealist Adventure plus Rio Moody Dancers. (Another Tempest fake?)
Sat Feb 10th- Bobby Johnson and the Atoms plus Vfranie.
Sat Feb 17th- Edwin Starr plus Motiv. (Another fake?)
Sat Feb 24th- Equals plus Magic Roundabout.
Sat Mar 2nd- Guy Hamilton Sound plus Sweet Heart.
Sat Mar 9th- Jimmy Cliff with Wynder K Frog, plus The Heretics.

Sat Mar 16ᵗʰ- Pesky Gee! plus The Trade.
Sat Mar 23ʳᵈ- Aynsley Dunbar Retaliation.
Sat Mar 30ᵗʰ- Chicken Shack with Christine Perfect.
Sat Apr 6ᵗʰ- La Pelle Nero plus Howling Robin and his Cool Cats Girls a go go.
Sun Apr 7ᵗʰ- The Symbols.
Sat Apr 13ᵗʰ- Riot Squad plus Blue Magnum.
Sat Apr 20ᵗʰ- Herbie Goins and the Nightimers, plus Howling Robin and his Cool Cats.
Sat Apr 27ᵗʰ- Showstoppers plus Rupert's Rick N Beckers (NO SHOW).
Sat May 4ᵗʰ- Nepenthe with backing group, plus The Trax.

The Trax from Rushden.

Sat May 11ᵗʰ- Hal C Blake plus Adlib plus Owlin Robin.
Sat May 18ᵗʰ- Savoy Brown Blues Band plus The Friction.

215

Sat May 25th- Skip Bifferty plus disco.

The Shopstoppers had split up and this band was sent in their place. They later became The Persuaders. Yet another of Roy Tempest's fakes.

Sat June 1st- Chantells plus Wild 'n Silk Band, Sue Spencer, Kirk St James. **Stage 2**- Simon K and the Meantimes.
Sat Jun 8th- Family.
Sat Jun 15th- The Taste plus Soul Bucket Show.
Sat Jun 22nd- Honeybus plus Art (from Leicester- John Deacon on bass)

Sat Jun 29ᵗʰ- Four Kents plus Submarines.
Sat Jul 6ᵗʰ- Freddie Fingers Lee plus Bubblegum.
Sat Jul 13ᵗʰ- Simon K & the Meantimers plus Trax.
Sat Jul 20ᵗʰ- Dr K's Big Blues Band, plus Rupert's Rick 'n Beckers.
Sat Jul 27ᵗʰ- Pesky Gee plus disco.
Sat Aug 3ʳᵈ- Jethro Tull.
Sat Aug 10ᵗʰ- Vanity Fair plus disco.
Sat Aug 17ᵗʰ- Aynsley Dunbar Retaliation.
Sat Aug 24ᵗʰ- Freddie Mac & Mac Sound.
Sat Aug 31ˢᵗ- Lloyd Alexander Real Estate plus Donnell Jackson & Broadway Crowd.
Sat Sep 7ᵗʰ- The Taste plus the CAT Roadshow with US Flattop.
Sat Sep 14ᵗʰ- Lucas and the Mike Cotton Sound.
Sat Sep 21ˢᵗ- Billy Davis plus Bubblegum.
Sat Sep 28ᵗʰ- Simon Dupree and the Big Sound, plus The Krisis.

Sat Oct 5th- Cuby and The Blizzards (from Holland), plus Simon K and the Meantimers.
Sat Oct 12th- Fearns Brass Foundry.
Sat Oct 19th- Foundations plus The Market.

Sat Oct 26th- Fantastics (USA) plus The Trax. (*They had previously played the Tin Hat as the Fabulous Temptations*)
Sat Nov 2nd- Fleetwood Mac, Duster Bennett, plus Chris Shakespears Globe Show.
Sat Nov 9th- Oscar Toney Junior plus Apex Big Roll Band.

Sat Nov 16th- Flirtations plus Chris Bartley & group.
Sat Nov 23rd- Black Cat Bones plus Bubblegum.
Sat Nov 20th- The Taste plus Sonny Burke Show.
Sat Dec 7th- JJ Jackson backed by Kippington Lodge.
Sat Dec 14th- The CAT Roadshow feat US Flattop.
Sat Dec 21st- Wynder K Frog.
Tue Dec 24th- New Formula.
Sat Dec 28th- Ferris Wheel? (no separate advert).
Tues Dec 31st- Bubblegum.

Tin Hat dates 1969.

Sat Jan 4th- Simon K & The Meantimers.
Sat Jan 11th- Radio1's Mike Raven plus Hal C. Blake.
Sat Jan 18th- Ray Williams and his Grenades.
Sat Jan 25th- Sasparella.

Sat Feb 1st- Plastic Penny.

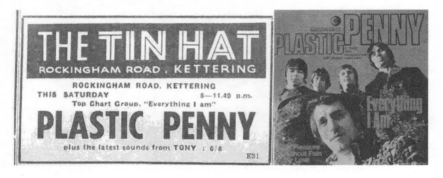

Sat Feb 8th- Paul Williams Set (Formerly the Alan Price Set).
Sat Feb 15th- 20th Century Show.

From February 22nd the adverts suggest that the venue had changed hands. The adverts have KAWMC printed on them. Had the club been taken over by the Kettering Athletic Working Mens Club? Within a few weeks the adverts had moved from the main entertainments page to the 'Around the clubs' page.

Sat Feb 22nd- (KAWMC) The Decoys & Disco.

Sat March 1st-(KAWMC) Simon K & Meantimers.
*Sat March 8th-*Closed for redecorating. Re-open April 5th.

The TIN HAT Club

ROCKINGHAM ROAD,
KETTERING

will be

CLOSED

FOR DECORATING

RE-OPEN APRIL 5th, 1969

THE TIN HAT

ROCKINGHAM ROAD . KETTERING

K.W.A.C.

RE-OPENING SATURDAY, APRIL 5th, 1969
WITH A 4-HOUR CONTINUOUS LIVE SHOW

THE SOUL EXPRESS

AN ALL COLOURED SIX PIECE

AND

THE KETAS

Line-up: Organ, Sax., Trumpet, Drums and Two Guitars
Members and Bona Fide Guests Only
Admission 6 6   ::   8—11.45

Sat April 5th- Soul Express plus The Ketas.
Sat April 12th- Noel & The Fireballs plus Shelley Tane.
Sat April 19th- Ruby James & Sound Trekkers.
Sat April 26th- Freddie Noaks & The Rudies, plus Herbal Remedy.
Weds April 30th- Disco every Weds.

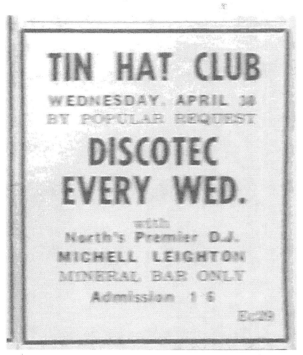

Sat May 3rd- Status Quo.
Sat May 10th- Killing Floor.
Sat May 17th- The Ebonies.
Fri May 23rd- Sand.
Sat May 24th- Jerome Arnold Band.
Sat May 31st- Scorpions.

June Mondays- TTT Disco.

Not quite chart-topping acts.

Fri June 6th- Discotet.
Sat June 7th- Mandrakes.
Sat June 14th- Wellington Kitch.

Sat June 21ˢᵗ- Moth.
Fri June 27ᵗʰ- Theodore Green.
Sat June 28ᵗʰ- The Variations.
July Fridays- TTT Disco.

Sat July 5ᵗʰ- Monday Morning Glory Band.
Sat July 12ᵗʰ- Simon K & Meantimers.
Sat July 19ᵗʰ- Ace Kefford Stand. (former Move bass player)
Sat July 26ᵗʰ- The Axe with Rodger Bloom.

A far cry from 1967 and John Mayall and Jethro Tull.

Sat August 2ⁿᵈ No Advert in paper
Sat Aug 9ᵗʰ- Cherry Blossom Clinic
Sat Aug 16ᵗʰ- Sand
Sat Aug 23ʳᵈ- Ptarmigen
Sat Aug 30ᵗʰ- Killing Floor

Sat Sept 6th- Clouds
Sat Sept 13th- Lions of Juda (from Israel)
Sat Sept 20th- Herd (after Peter Frampton had left them)
Sat Sept 27th- Pink Cheeks

Sat Oct 4th- Epics
Sat Oct 11th- Moth
Sat Oct 18th- Max Romeo
Sat Oct 25th- Orange Bicycle

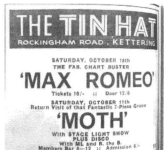

Sat Nov 1ˢᵗ- J J Jackson
Sat Nov 8ᵗʰ- Solid State Stereo Disco
Sat Nov 15ᵗʰ- Shirelles
Sat Nov 22ⁿᵈ- Freddie Mac
Sat Nov 29ᵗʰ- no advert

Sat Dec 6ᵗʰ- No advert
Sat Dec 13ᵗʰ- Diary
Sat Dec 20ᵗʰ- Disco
Weds Dec 24ᵗʰ- Moth
Fri Dec 26ᵗʰ- Smoke
Weds Dec 31ˢᵗ- Barabus & Sand

1969. The end of an era.
No mention of the Tompkins or Dobson families?

APPENDIX 2: BEFORE THEY WERE FAMOUS

The beat music boom began in earnest in 1963. There was a huge demand for bands to play the latest hits and a network of venues sprang up across the country. Most of the bands who toured up and down the country are long forgotten, but many of the superstars of the 70s learned their trade with them. Here are a few adverts from the Evening Telegraph of 1963-68. Did the people who watched these groups realise who they were seeing on that stage?

April 1963. Jimmy Page was Neil's lead guitarist in the early 1960s. Deep Purple's Richie Blackmore also played with him in 1965.

This gig was a few days before the group were booked for the Beatles Christmas Show at Finsbury Park Astoria (later the Rainbow). They scored their first hit a few months later. In the 1970s they recorded all their albums at Derek's Beck Studio in Wellingborough.

Their lead guitarist was Jeff Beck. He joined the Yardbirds when Eric Clapton left.

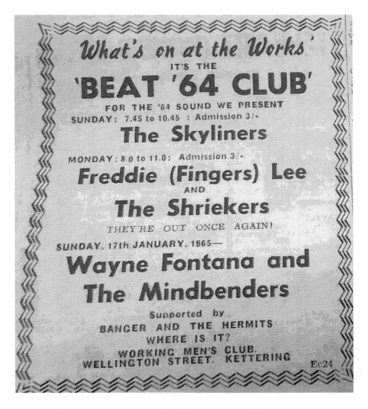

Future 10cc guitarist Eric Stewart was a Mindbender.

The King Bees were drummer Carl Palmer's first group.

A young David Jones (David Bowie) was a member of this group in January 65.

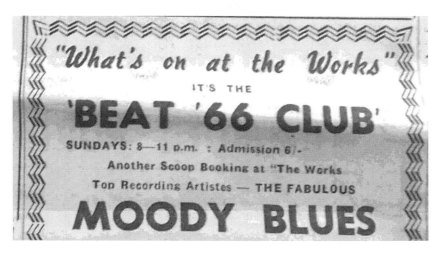

Wings co-founder Denny Laine was their lead vocalist/guitarist. Justin Hayward replaced him soon after this booking.

David 'Lord' Sutch later founded the Monster Raving Looney Party, Future Deep Purple star Richie Blackmore was his lead guitarist at this show.

Dean Ford and The Gaylords - now professional

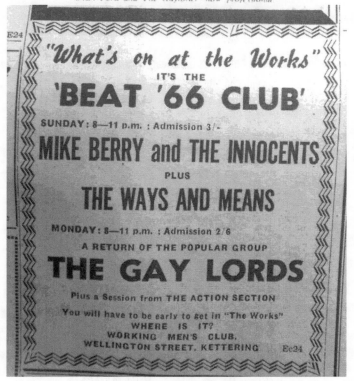

"What's on at the Works"
IT'S THE
'BEAT '66 CLUB'
SUNDAY: 8—11 p.m. : Admission 3/-
MIKE BERRY and THE INNOCENTS
PLUS
THE WAYS AND MEANS
MONDAY: 8—11 p.m. : Admission 2/6
A RETURN OF THE POPULAR GROUP
THE GAY LORDS
Plus a Session from THE ACTION SECTION
You will have to be early to get in "The Works"
WHERE IS IT?
WORKING MEN'S CLUB,
WELLINGTON STREET, KETTERING   Ec24

In 1965 The Gaylords moved down from Scotland and lodged with relatives in Corby.
Soon after this booking they changed their name to Marmalade. They were regulars at
the Works. They scored their first hit in 1968 with 'Lovin' Things'.

January 1967. Mud were regulars at this venue. Their early singles flopped, and it wasn't until they signed to Mickie Most's Rak label in the early 70s that they had chart success. 'Tiger Feet' was the UK's best-selling single of 1974.

May 6th, 1967. The Spectres changed their name to Status Quo soon after this show and went on to become one of the world's top bands. The Jigsaw was formed in 1965. In 1975 they had a top 10 hit with 'Sky High'. Drummer /vocalist Des Dyer still performs regularly with Steve Fearn in a duo called Fingersnfumbs.

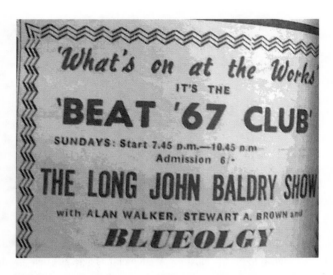

The show took place a few months before the release of his number one single 'Let the Heartaches Begin'. Bluesology's piano player was 20-year-old Reg Dwight. He changed his name to Elton John (named after sax player Elton Dean and singer John Baldry). And the rest is history.

The GBO's past band members included Jack Bruce and Ginger Baker. This line up featured Dick Heckstall-Smith on saxophone, Jon Hiseman on drums and John McLaughlin on guitar. In 1974 a penniless Bond took his own life by jumping in front of a tube train.

The future Led Zeppelin vocalist played Higham Ferrers WMC on July 13th, 1967.

Alexis Korner was a great encourager of young musicians. His backing musicians on this date included future members of Free who went on to score a worldwide hit with 'All Right Now'.

The Cheynes were one of the Rolling Stones' supporting acts when they played Kettering in 1964. The lanky youth at the back was 19-year-old Mick Fleetwood, founder member of Fleetwood Mac. The boy dun good!

If you enjoyed reading this book, you may be interested in these other titles. Firstly- Mavis has written her own story. First published in 2005, it contains many of the stories we included in 'Back Street Genius' but are told from her viewpoint. It's a thoroughly enjoyable and engaging read.

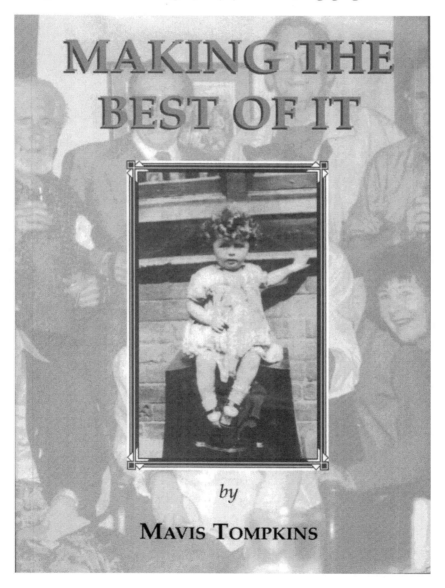

MAKING THE BEST OF IT

by

MAVIS TOMPKINS

Mavis still has a few copies available at a discount price. Please contact us for more details.

THIS is the journal of a Kettering girl, as she recalls some of the events and happenings that occurred in her life from the thirties up to the year 2000, and also that of her father's, Cyril Charles Dobson, an inventive and entrepreneurial engineer.

Interwoven within these memories, she tells a fascinating story that begins with her father's own anecdotes. Born in Wellington Street in 1908, we learn of his close escape from drowning in the Ise Brook, the childhood pranks he played; his first experiments with the then 'new' electricity; love and romance in the jazz age, and realising his ultimate ambition, to run his own business – The Cytringan Electric Welding Company.

In 1943, despite the shortages of wartime, he built a thirty foot steel boat in his back garden – a unique project in which his family and factory workers all took part, culminating in trips on the River Nene and across The Wash in the North Sea, and in 1959 he successfully patented a combined arc welder, battery booster and trickle charger.

One of his enduring characteristics was his determination to overcome any obstacle, (with as little expense as possible), and his unwillingness to conform to rules and regulations.

The author recalls her home and childhood in Cambridge Street, throughout WW2 and peacetime, schooldays and playtime; the 'invasion' of the 'Yanks' in our county of Northamptonshire; teenage love and life in the forties and fifties; adventures on the good ship 'Cytringan', and a marriage fraught with the difficulties of running a home and shop. She remembers the 'Swinging Sixties'- local rock groups, musicians, and the hopefuls who came to her husband Derek's recording studios, along with some of the famous. One of these 'hopefuls' eventually became a top music/record producer for Warner Brothers of Los Angeles, David Foster. He never forgot the advice given by Derek, and in the year 2000 David invited him and his wife Mavis over to stay at his 22 acre Malibu estate for a couple of weeks.

The town of Kettering and it's county, together with some of its colourful inhabitants, a few unsung heroes, some famous and some eccentric, is remembered throughout those years with humour and affection, and among these recollections must flow times of sadness and tears, but also much laughter and moments of sheer hilarity.

A reflection of how her father influenced her own character, unwittingly bestowing the author with the stubborn will to carry on regardless, reminded her of how they all, throughout those precious years, 'made the best of it'

£15.95

Dave Clemo has had several books published including three volumes of his musical autobiography. The first volume covers his early life in Cornwall, his family's move to London in 1962 and spending his teenage years in the epicentre of the Underground music scene which was centred on Ladbroke Grove in West London. It ends when he moved to Northampton in 1974.

Dave's books are all available in Kindle Format.

We live in an age where we are surrounded by music. It's everywhere, but it wasn't always thus. As a young boy, growing up in Cornwall in the 1950's, Dave Clemo was too young for rock n roll. There was no music on the radio (as strange as that seems) and MTV was part of the sci-fi generation.

Fast forward ten years and the world had changed. Dave had changed with it. Now living in West London, he was part of the underground scene, when Pink Floyd still had 'The' at the start of their name and Jimi Hendrix arrived from America like a whirlwind. Dave saw Floyd and Hendrix perform as well as King Crimson, Jethro Tull, the Who, Genesis and every band that would go onto stardom in the 60's and 70's.

Emulating them, Dave learnt to play the guitar and became a stalwart of the London music scene, without ever hitting the heights of his heroes. For history to become folklore, someone has to witness it. 'Too Young For Rock n Roll' is an eyewitness account of the birth of rock, prog and folk music in Britain. A feast for your ears and your eyes.

ISBN 978-1-911559-46-7

£14.99

9 781911 559467

The second volume covers the years up to 1984, and his time as a founder member of Northampton based rock group Left Hand Drive. They were caught between the end of the prog rock era and the emerging punk rock scene when he left them in 1976 to form a covers band that played the local clubs for the next five years.

Dave's books are all available in Kindle Format.

DAVE CLEMO

TOO OLD FOR PUNK

Since I first picked up a guitar and attempted to play a chord I've been motivated by a desire to improve and develop as a player. It might be argued that we musicians are indifferent to the audience. We appreciate them being there and the times when the band and the audience gel into a whole make it worthwhile. To coin a phrase, it strikes a chord.

As far as I was concerned, playing three chords and pogoing while trying to dodge the spittle from the audience was not a progression. I was not interested.

Listen to 'Anarchy in the UK', then listen to Steely Dan's 'Josie'.
Which song offers the biggest challenge to the musician?

People tell me that Punk is a state of mind.

I was too old for that.

ISBN 978-1-911559-65-6

£14.99

9 781911 559658

The third volume brings his story up to date and covers his emergence as a singer/songwriter and recording artiste who has released a dozen or more albums to date. He also taught himself the bass guitar and played on several national tours of theatres, festivals and clubs, most notably as part of Nicki Gillis' UK touring band. It also chronicles the various health issues he has had to content with, and the way it has shaped his current musical activities.

Also available in Kindle Format.

Contact Dave if you're interested in any of these books

daveclemo@live dot com

In the late 60's and early 70's Roger Kinsey was heavily involved in the music business, running a Cambridge based Entertainments Agency and Music Management business called Rufus Manning Associates. He is planning to produce a book about those days that will include his involvement in organising and promoting what is now recognised as being the world's first ever 4-day FREE Music Festival, held on Midsummer Common in early June 1969. His company also sponsored the second FREE Festival held over two days in August 1970 on Coldhams Common.

He is also researching two more books for future publication. The first will document the stories and history of the assorted venues around the East Northants area from the late 50s through to the late 70s, and the groups who played them, some of whom went on to greater things.

The other book will tell the story of how Big Bob Knight along with Steve Hadjuk and others put the legendary Nags Head pub in Wollaston on the musical map. This venue pioneered Blues and Soul Nights in the late 60s and early 70s. The legendary radio presenter and DJ John Peel had a residency and Rod Stewart and The Faces, Alexis Korner and the future members of Free all played memorable shows. Big Bob's nights at the Nags drew crowds from miles around.

Roger would love to hear from anyone who has fond memories of these events and would like to contribute to the book. Second-hand ones from perhaps your parents or even grandparents would also be welcome!

Any photos or other ephemera/memorabilia always welcome and everyone contributing will be acknowledged.

Contact him via email- plum54kinsey@btinternet.com

Or via Facebook.com/Roger Chris Kinsey.

The follow up to 'Back Street Genius' is currently being researched. We are gathering information from a variety of sources including interviews with many of the musicians who recorded at Beck. Our aim is to make these volumes the definitive history of Derek's legacy and how he impacted the music scene both locally and nationally.